The Tennyson Album

The Tennyson Album

A biography in original photographs

by Andrew Wheatcroft

Introduction by Sir John Betjeman

Routledge & Kegan Paul
London, Boston and Henley

For Janet,
in love and gratitude

First published in 1980
by Routledge & Kegan Paul Ltd
39 Store Street, London WC1E 7DD,
Broadway House, Newtown Road,
Henley-on-Thames, Oxon RG9 1EN and
9 Park Street, Boston, Mass. 02108, USA

British Library Cataloguing in Publication Data

Tennyson album.

1. Tennyson, Alfred, Baron Tennyson –
Portraits, etc.
2. Poets, English – 19th century – Portraits
I. Wheatcroft, Andrew
821'.8   PR5585   80–40021

ISBN 0 7100 0494 X

Set in Photina
Filmset and printed in Great Britain by
BAS Printers Limited, Over Wallop, Hampshire

Contents

Preface and acknowledgments

TENNYSON HAD little time for biography unless, as he said, 'it is done by one who wholly loves the man whose life he writes, yet loves him with a discriminating love.' In his first biographer, his son Hallam, love was all-embracing, but discrimination in smaller measure. In the many works of the poet's grandson, Sir Charles Tennyson, the balance was restored and we can now see Tennyson as a more human and scarcely less grand figure. The intention of this book is to show by means of original photographs both the grandeur and humanity of Tennyson's character, as seen by those who knew him. All the photographs in this volume are contemporary, save two; the two modern photographs, of Harrington Hall and Aldworth, illustrate aspects of the houses ignored by earlier photographers. In the text which accompanies them I have sought where possible to use the words of Tennyson, his family, friends and contemporaries, rather than interpolate my own.

Few English poets have toppled from such heights of general acclaim into such an abyss of disregard. Even today, Tennyson can be relied upon as a comedian's hardy perennial: 'Come into the garden, Maud' is an old favourite. The power and subtlety of his poetry is often veiled and it has taken the masterly dissection to be found in Christopher Ricks's critical biography to reveal his 'unclamorous claim to the central humanity of a great poet'.

I am indebted to Her Majesty The Queen for Her gracious permission to reproduce material from the Royal Archives. Without the kindness of Lord Tennyson and the co-operation of the Tennyson Research Centre in Lincoln, who have given free access to their large collection, this volume would not have been possible, and I am also grateful to the Librarian and Staff of the Louth Library, for their ready assistance with material from their local collection. The University Library, Cambridge, and the London Library have proved unfailingly helpful. One of the most pleasant mornings in the preparation of this book was spent with Lady Maitland at Harrington Hall, and without her help I should never have found a satisfactory photograph of Harrington. Alan Le Cras produced unlikely volumes from his library in answer to obscure queries, and I am grateful to him. C. V. Middleton & Son, Photographers, of Lincoln, showed considerable expertise in copying old photographs, and I would like to thank them.

Finally, there are three people whose contribution to the volume is manifest in the finished product. Sir John Betjeman has provided the introduction, but his influence has ranged far more widely. His passion for Tennyson, his house in Chelsea with volumes by 'The Bard' propped in odd corners, a print of Julia Margaret Cameron's portrait of 'The Dirty Monk' leaning casually against a cabinet, has shaped my approach to the book. He encouraged my enthusiasms, insisted that we read Tennyson to each other, and in general pressed the enterprise towards its conclusion. Laurence Elvin, FSA, FRHistS, was until his recent retirement, Librarian, Local History and Tennyson Collections, Lincolnshire Library Service. He knows more about photographs of Tennyson than any man alive. His encyclopaedic knowledge, insistence on quality, and complete readiness to share his experience has made him the keystone of the enterprise, and a good friend.

Without the advice and help of my wife Janet, I should, no doubt, have finished this book in half the time; it would also have been wholly unsatisfactory. The idea of the book was hers, born of her walks to Somersby and her passion for Tennyson. If she has failed to make me less sedentary, I have at least caught her enthusiasm for the poet. This book engendered innumerable arguments and the many imperfections which remain are evidence of my invincible stubborness and refusal to accept her advice. I am deeply grateful to her.

Andrew Wheatcroft
Hagg Newhall
Lincolnshire

Introduction
SIR JOHN BETJEMAN

Tennyson had a wonderful ear for the sound of words, a keen eye for detail, and a lovely dry humour. I wish I had known him. This book is wanted, for it brings the Tennysons as a family striding out of Lincolnshire, that too-little appreciated county, into the rest of the world.

Tennyson was very much a family man, loved by his children and grandchildren. He was like a big friendly dog and treated as such by them. He always kept large dogs about him, which followed him as he walked, or slumped by his chair in his study when he worked. He was lucky in his family, not just his wife and sons, but all his brothers and sisters as well; his wife, Emily, was his secretary and second self. 'June Bracken and Heather' is his glorious tribute to their marriage.

> There on the top of the down,
> The wild heather round me and over me June's high blue,
> When I looked at the bracken so bright and the heather so brown,
> I thought to myself I would offer this book to you,
> This, and my love together,
> To you that are seventy seven,
> With a faith as clear as the heights of the June-blue heaven
> And a fancy as summer-new
> As the green of the bracken and the gloom of the heather.

Hallam Tennyson, his son, wrote a reverent memoir of his father which is still readable and full of Tennyson humour. *Tennyson and his friends*, which Hallam edited, tells us even more. But the person who told us most was Tennyson's grandson, Sir Charles Tennyson. He lifted, for ever, off the great poet the mists of uncritical hero worship and brought about the reconciliation of the families of Tennyson d'Eyncourt in Bayons Manor and the rector's children of Somersby.

In the 1920s, when I was young, Tennyson was laughed off as an old-fashioned, Victorian poet and equated with the American, Longfellow. Slowly he has climbed back to the eminence where he should be, right at the top. Lord David Cecil told me that two great peaks rise either side of English Victorian poetry. The beginning is Wordsworth and the end is Hardy. I agree. But where is Tennyson in between them? He is a broad river flowing through a rich meadow. He is as strong as Wordsworth and less gloomy than Hardy's village fatalism. He is a country gentleman with a country gentleman's taste of those days in art. He liked Latin and Greek, in which he was well grounded by his clever, nervous father, and the Elizabethan style in architecture. His courage and breadth of vision come out in one of his last and most beautiful poems, which fulfils, for me, all his early promise, 'Early Spring':

Once more the Heavenly Power
Makes all things new,
And domes the red-plowed hills
With loving blue;
The blackbirds have their wills,
The throstles too.

Opens a door in Heaven;
From skies of glass
A Jacob's ladder falls
On greening grass,
And o'er the mountain-walls
Young angels pass.

Before them fleets the shower,
And burst the buds,
And shine the level lands,
And flash the floods;
The stars are from their hands
Flung through the woods,

The woods with living airs
How softly fanned,
Light airs from where the deep,
All down the sand,
Is breathing in his sleep,
Heard by the land.

O follow, leaping blood,
The season's lure!
O heart, look down and up
Serene, secure,
Warm as the crocus cup,
Like snowdrops, pure!

Past, Future glimpse and fade
Through some slight spell
A gleam from yonder vale,
Some far blue fell,
And sympathies, how frail,
In sound and smell!

Till at thy chuckled note,
Thou twinkling bird,
The fairy fancies range,
And, lightly stirred,
Ring little bells of change
From word to word.

For now the Heavenly Power
Makes all things new,
And thaws the cold, and fills
The flower with dew;
The blackbirds have their wills,
The poets too.

There have been some good books on Tennyson's country, whether in the Isle of Wight, Surrey, or his native Lincolnshire. So far as illustrations are concerned the best of these was published in 1905 by A. & C. Black and called *The Homes of Tennyson*. The pictures were water-colours by Helen Allingham. Her husband William was the poet and friend of Tennyson. But what has not been turned to until now has been the aid of photography. Mrs Cameron's photographs have an unearthly quality and show Tennyson's friends and relations as though they were alive now and not under the ground in Lincolnshire, the Isle of Wight, Surrey, or Highgate cemetery.

A favourite artist of Tennyson was his friend Edward Lear, now chiefly known for his Nonsense Poems, but then famous as a painter of the Mediterranean and birds. Andrew Wheatcroft says that Tennyson loathed the Moxon illustrated edition of his poems, with engravings from paintings by the Pre-Raphaelites. Their version of the Middle Ages was certainly not Tennyson's. Aldworth and the Tudor style of the 1840s were to Tennyson's taste: his favourite colours seemed to have been greens and browns.

Tennyson was always interested in science and astronomy. Anyone who reads his poem 'Vastness' can grasp his sense of things outside the human race. The stars comforted him, with their great distances from each other. Nature delighted him with its detail, e.g. 'Ruddy-hearted blossom flake about the flowers of an elm tree'. He liked the sea being round him, and particularly the North Sea. There are some lines in the 'The Last Tournament' which I like to remember by heart . . .

> . . . as the crest of some slow-arching wave
> Heard in dead night along that table-shore
> Drops flat, and after the great waters break
> Whitening for half a league, and thin themselves,
> Far over sands marbled with moon and cloud,
> From less and less to nothing; thus he fell
> Head-heavy . . .

Though it may sound like ending this introduction with the conclusion of an after-dinner speech, I feel honoured to be associated with this book. It is worthy of its subject.

JOHN BETJEMAN

'. . . another set of Tennyson pictures.
Rather sickening these semblances
of biography which are no biography . . .'

Emily Tennyson to her sister Anne, June 1890

The wolds of Lincolnshire, where Alfred Tennyson was born and spent his formative years, remain an isolated and little-known corner of England. Its hills which rise, unexpectedly, from the flat lands of the fen have never experienced the domination of the great estates and quasi-feudal landowners. The people who a century ago still spoke a dialect impenetrable to outsiders were energetic, intractable and unruly; small wonder therefore, that Henry VIII, beset by the Lincolnshire Rebellion, had castigated the Woldsmen, calling them:

The most brute and beastly of the whole realm . . .

The Tennysons, although their origins lay across the Humber in Yorkshire, had begun to establish themselves in the Wolds when Alfred's grandfather purchased an estate in 1783 on the rising land above the village of Tealby, a manor with the romantic connotations of having once belonged to the great mediaeval family of d'Eyncourt, from whom he traced a rather tenuous descent. It is perhaps excessive to draw too close a line of connection between environment and character, yet the Tennysons soon came to embody the traits of the Woldsmen. George Tennyson, the purchaser of Bayons Manor at Tealby, was a successful lawyer, an expert in the legal complexities of land enclosure, and thus the confidant of the leading county families. Proud and unbending, he was respected, even feared, by his clients; towards his family, he intended to be a patriarch and the founder of a landed dynasty. He married Mary Turner, from a family living near by at Caistor, in 1775; two daughters, Elizabeth and Mary, were born in 1776 and 1777, and their first son in the following year. He was named George Clayton, after his father.

The birth of a son to so convinced a dynast as George Tennyson assumed great importance, which makes all the more extraordinary his behaviour towards the boy. Mary and George Clayton were barely out of infancy before they were bundled off to grandparents, in Caistor and Holderness, to be brought up away from home; Elizabeth, the favourite of both her parents, remained with them. It was as if George could only lavish his affection on a single object, and from the birth of his second son, Charles, in 1784, all his hopes for the future were focused upon him. George Clayton was probably a self-willed child, a little unlovable; even his mother said: 'I think I never saw a child so rude and ungovernable.' But it is a measure of George Tennyson's ambition and his cold determination to establish his family among the élite of the county that he was prepared to discard his elder son, and to use Charles as the vehicle for his social and political ambitions. He outlined this plan to a neighbouring squire, who replied robustly: 'George, if you do this you'll certainly be damned, you will indeed.' The curse, in the event, fell not upon George Tennyson, the 'old man of the Wolds' as his grandchildren were to refer to him, in a neat and rather precocious allusion to the Old Man of the Mountains, chief of the Assassins, but upon his children and their descendants.

The striking resemblance between the two Tennyson brothers, evident in their portraits, disguises the variance in their characters. The notable beauty of the Tennysons, which their sister Elizabeth described in Charles as 'his Charles I countenance', had a stronger, more powerful, even brutal quality in George Clayton. His wildness grew with age: at Cambridge he was often in trouble with the college authorities on account of his idleness and insubordination; news of his behaviour filtered back to his father. On one notable occasion, he even fired a pistol ball through the window of Trinity College Chapel, but, miraculously, was not discovered. These reports served only to reinforce his father's decision to use Charles in his scheme for the rise of the family to power and fortune. While his second son was still in the schoolroom, he had made preparations for the elder boy, by now at St John's College, Cambridge, to enter the Church, a career for which he had displayed no aptitude or concern; in 1801 George Clayton was ordained a deacon, and some eighteen months later took priest's orders. In the interim, he had visited Russia, at his father's expense, and there underwent by his own account a series of adventures so improbable as to border on fantasy. His son Alfred later repeated the tale to his wife, and it is recorded in her *Journal*:

A told the thrilling story of his father's stay in Russia: how, as a very young man, he was dining with our English Minister, Lord St. Helens, at St. Petersburg, when he said, across a Russian, to Lord St. Helens, 'It is perfectly well known in England who murdered the Emperor Paul: it was Count So and So.' Whereat a dead silence fell on the company. After dinner Lord St. Helens called Dr. Tennyson aside and said, 'Ride for your life from this city; the man across whom you were speaking to me was the Count So and So, whom you accused of murdering the Emperor Paul.' Dr. Tennyson took horse and rode for weeks and weeks through Russia, till he came to the Crimea where he fell ill. He became delirious, and remembered the wild country-people dancing round his bed with magical incantations. Once in every three months an English courier passed through this village where he lay ill, and as he passed through the village blew a horn. It all depended on Dr. Tennyson's hearing this horn whether he could escape from Russia, for he had no money. In his delirium he would perpetually start up agonized lest he had missed it. At last the courier came, the horn was blown and he heard the sound, and applied to the courier to take him. The courier agreed, and Dr. Tennyson journeyed with him.

In this bizarre anecdote, George Clayton is cast as hero; life at home promised only a settled monotony. In 1805, he married a local beauty, Elizabeth Fytche, a daughter of the Rector of the town of Louth, and his father engineered two more parishes — Somersby and Bag Enderby — to add to his benefice at Benniworth. The income from them, with an annual allowance of £140 from George Tennyson, allowed them to live without financial anxiety. The new Rector of Somersby and Bag Enderby moved into his rectory at Somersby in 1808 after bitter arguments over repairs and extensions to the house; by then he had a family of two young sons. The third, Alfred, was born at Somersby on 6 August 1809. Eight more children were to follow, at approximately annual intervals; Elizabeth Tennyson bore a child every year from 1806 to 1819, save in 1812, 1814, 1818. All of these children, except the first, George, who died in infancy, survived to adulthood. Life for George Clayton came to assume a troublesome pattern: an increasing family, and its consequent financial problems, lack of preferment in the Church, and a growing sense of resentment at his treatment by his father. Even the pleasures of his early years at Somersby, when he was building a fine library, dazzling local society with his ebullience and intellect, even the scholarly delights of teasing out the problems of theology in his finely honed sermons dimmed as the years passed. That he felt his talents frustrated is byond doubt. The rectory at Somersby, absurdly small for a family of thirteen, was set in a small and primitive village; Bag Enderby was a mere hamlet. The Tennysons were thought mad by the parish; their cook remarked, in Alfred's hearing, 'If you raäked out Hell with a smaäll tooth coämb you weän't find their likes.' Of the Doctor's exquisite sermons (George Clayton took a degree of Doctor of Civil Laws in 1813) one parishioner in later years only remembered 'E read 'em from a paäper and I didn't know what 'e meant.' At one time he had enjoyed the annual visits which he made to Cambridge with his brother Charles, finding there the conversation and stimulus lacking in Lincolnshire, but he approached middle age with foreboding and increasing morbidity. Progressively, the 'black blood of the Tennysons', a tendency to savage depression which also afflicted, in a different measure, 'The Old Man of the Wolds', and Charles Tennyson, came to rule his personality.

below

Charles Tennyson d'Eyncourt (1784–1861), about 1810
John Harrison

The career of Charles Tennyson d'Eyncourt was outwardly more successful than that of his elder brother. Elected to Parliament in 1818 for Grimsby, and later, the victor of an epic battle for the seat at Stamford, a Privy Councillor from 1832, and an ardent advocate of parliamentary reform, he never achieved either the political success or the title he coveted. His baronial fantasy of Bayons embodied all his desires to show the antiquity and honour of his lineage, the seat of a *Lord* d'Eyncourt, or at the least, a *Sir Charles* d'Eyncourt. He was to achieve neither. Failure soured him, and the death of his favourite son turned him towards a morose distaste for all around him. His less favoured children he referred to as the The Sot, The Shrew, The Snob, and

The Stone, and even his greatest achievement, his 'idyll in stone' Bayons Manor, was damned. In his last years he is supposed to have driven through the great park he had lovingly created, to a point where he could look down on the turrets and roofs of the house; 'I must have been mad' was his only comment.

right

George Clayton Tennyson (1778–1831), about 1812

The inferior quality of this portrait, compared with his brother's (*opposite*), is mute evidence of their relative status in society. But their similarity in appearance is striking, and in character they had much in common. In George Clayton, the rough edges of his nature were unrounded, and he had little of the easy civility which carried his brother far in London drawing rooms.

above

Elizabeth Tennyson, *née* Fytche (1781–1865)

'One of the most angelick natures on God's earth',
Elizabeth was idolised by all her children; she gave them
the constant, unquestioning affection which their father
could not provide. The Fytches were a well-connected
family; George Clayton did well in his marriage, for she
was a noted beauty, who had already refused twenty-
five proposals of matrimony. Her affection for him, even
in his derangement, was constant, and her warm-
heartedness extended to all around her. She loved
animals, keeping a pet monkey, occasional birds, and a
bevy of other livestock. It was held among the rougher
lads of Somersby and Bag Enderby that the easiest way
to earn a penny was to beat a dog under her window,
for she would assuredly pay you to stop. Yet she was
capable of a tart retort, and a spirited resistance to
slights on her family. In later years, in the many houses
that the Tennysons occupied, she presided over an
increasingly uncouth and eccentric household with a
sublime indifference.

right

Somersby Rectory, about 1889

Although the rectory was rebuilt and improved before
they moved in, Dr Tennyson enlarged the house to
accommodate his burgeoning family. In 1819, with the
help of the redoubtable Horlins (who once, on being
reprimanded by the Doctor for not cleaning the carriage
harness, hurled it at his master's feet and told him to
clean it himself), he built the 'Gothic Hall' at the right of
the photograph; a bricklayer was called in, one
suspects, to remedy the defects. As a craftsman in wood
Dr Tennyson was far superior, and the house was
decorated with his fine carving; it was a talent which
Alfred inherited.

18

IFE AT Somersby was ruled by the Doctor's moods and passions, yet the prevailing atmosphere was of happiness and excitement rather than gloom. George Clayton made few allowances for his children, but, in exchange, he allowed them most of the privileges of adulthood. His library was open to them, the collection of a scholar and bibliophile, especially in those fields which chiefly interested him, history, travel, and the great classic authors in Latin and Greek; many of the books are adorned with doodles in Alfred's hand. Conversation at Somersby was continuous and often raucous; the children played games on the lawns around the house, as well as in the fields and woods of the village, wild and complex rituals which bemused the villagers:

they were 'champions and warriors, defending a field, or a stone-heap, or again they would set up opposing camps with a king in the midst of each. The king was a willow-wand stuck into the ground, with an outer circle of immortals, to defend him, or firmer, stiffer sticks. Then each party would come with stones, hurling at each other's king and trying to overthrow him.'

As they grew older, they travelled more regularly to dances and celebrations in Spilsby and Horncastle, as their parents had done before them. They quickly made a mark among the families of the neighbourhood. Sophie Rawnsley, a daughter of the Rector of Halton Holgate, a close friend of Dr Tennyson, was struck by Alfred:

We liked to talk better than to dance together at Horncastle or Spilsby or Halton; he always had something worth saying and said it so quaintly. Most girls were frightened of him. I was never afraid of the man, but of his mind.

In later years, his wife used to tell her sons:

At your father's home, Somersby, we used to have evenings of music and singing. Your Aunt Mary played on the harp as her father used to do. She was a splendid looking girl, and would have made a beautiful picture. Then your aunt Emily (beloved of Arthur Hallam) had wonderful eyes — depths on depths they seemed to have—and a fine profile . . . All the brothers and sisters were to fair to see. Your father was kingly, masses of fine, wavy hair, very dark, with a pervading shade of gold, and long as it was then worn.

Alfred in those days must have looked much as he is portrayed by Samuel Lawrence or Annie Dixon. A Cambridge friend, W. H. Brookfield, remarked to him: 'Alfred, it isn't fair that you should be both Hercules and Apollo', and his extraordinary strength was remarkable even among the brawny yeomen and farmhands of the Wolds. He could, it

above left
The Devil

*From a sketchbook of Arthur and Horatio
Tennyson*

above
St Margaret's Church, Bag Enderby, summer
1890

This is the second, and smaller, of Dr Tennyson's
churches. Built in 1407, it dominated a tiny cluster of
cottages and a small manor house. The old parish clerk
was struck by the way the Tennyson girls were 'young
ladies who were never seen without a book in their
hands. . . . The Doctor war äll for reading. . . .'

22

Brothers in misery

left

The Wild Boy
From Arthur Tennyson's sketchbook

The 'queerish looking lad' is very reminiscent of the shaggy, dirty Tennyson boys in their later years at Somersby; Arthur often made rapid sketches of his brothers or the neighbouring families.

right

Brothers in misery, with Alfred (*left*) and Charles (*right*)
Arthur Tennyson

This wryly humorous sketch catches the deep misery for all in the rectory during Dr Tennyson's recurrent bouts of depression. It also shows the style of clothes which both Alfred and Charles, with no regard for taste or fashion, were to wear throughout their lives.

overleaf

Bag Enderby, 1889

The founder of Methodism, and another Lincolnshire notable John Wesley, preached under this tree, so village legend claimed, and the Tennyson daughters used to hang swings from its branches.

seemed, 'hurl the crow bar further than any of the neighbouring clowns . . .', yet he carried his great, muscular frame with grace, if not elegance: he was notorious for being illkempt, 'down on his heels and his coat unlaced and his hair anyhow. He was a rough un was Mister Halfred and no mistake . . .'

Alfred, because of his later fame, was no doubt better remembered than would otherwise have been the case, but his brothers and sisters were also remarkable. For the most part, tall and dark, they clearly stood together as a clan against the rest of the world. The daughter of another Lincolnshire contemporary later recalled them:

Tennysons are not easy to describe. There was both a natural grandeur and simplicity about them; a streak of impish mischief and a love of the gruesome. Delightfully unconventional, they were never like ordinary people; even their dress and walk seemed different.

The three elder Tennyson brothers, Frederick, Charles and Alfred, formed the natural apex of the family. They shared the same attic room in the crowded rectory, and possessed a remarkable identity of interests. Later in life, Frederick recalled how: 'I and Charles, and Alfred used to play at being Emperors of China, each appropriating a portion of the old echoing garden [at their Aunt Mary's house in Louth] as our domain, and making them reverberate our tones of authority.' Dr Tennyson was insistent that his own firstborn son should have those benefits which had been withheld from him. With the agreement of 'The Old Man of the Wolds', Frederick was sent to Eton; moreover, he was made heir to the considerable property of his Clayton ancestors in Grimsby. At Eton he proved a natural games player, both at cricket and football, but he also showed the independence and truculence of his nature; in appearance, closest of the family to his father, it seemed he had inherited his character as well. When he entered St John's College, Cambridge in 1826, he

23

continued to resist authority, so much so that a friend described him as 'sinister in aspect and terrific in manner, even to the discomfiture of elderly dons'.

With Frederick's departure for Eton, the natural leader of the family was removed, and Charles and Alfred flourished in his absence. Although they suffered a few miserable years at Louth Grammar School, under the Rev. J. Waite, a cousin of their mother, and 'a tempestuous flogging master of the old stamp', they were thereafter educated by their father at home. Despite his increasingly uncertain temper, and a growing resort to alcohol, he was an inspiring if exacting teacher. He encouraged his sons in writing both prose and poetry, criticising forthrightly but constructively. Alfred recalled in 1890 how: 'My father once said to me "Don't write so rhythmically, break your lines occasionally for the sake of variety."' His output was prodigious:

When I was about eight years old, I covered two sides of a slate with Thomsonian blank verse in praise of flowers for my brother Charles, who was a year older than I was, Thomson then being the only poet I knew. Before I could read, I was in the habit on a stormy day of spreading my arms to the wind, and crying out, 'I hear a voice that's speaking in the wind,' and the words 'far, far away' had always a strange charm for me . . . At about twelve and onward I wrote an epic of six thousand lines à la Walter Scott—full of battles, dealing too with sea and mountain scenery,—with Scott's regularity of octo-syllables and his occasional varieties. Though the performance was very likely worth nothing I never felt myself more truly inspired, I wrote as much as seventy lines at one time, and used to go shouting them about the fields in the dark. Somewhat later (at fourteen) I wrote a Drama in blank verse, which I have still, and other things. It seems to me, I wrote them all in perfect metre.

Dr Tennyson clearly realised his potential, remarking with pride, 'If Alfred die, one of our greatest poets will have gone'. Even his grandfather, to whom he gave a poem in memory of his grandmother, Mary, who died in 1825, was gruffly appreciative: 'Here is half a guinea for you, the first you have ever earned by poetry, and, take my word for it, the last . . . .' Within two years, Alfred was to prove him wrong, and the brothers crossed the frontier between 'shouting and holloaing and preaching', in the words of an old Somersby servant, and the dignity of published verse. For the volume, *Poems by Two Brothers*, published in 1827, they received, in cash, £10, and with some of it they hired a carriage, driving the fourteen miles to Mablethorpe (where they had spent several happy holidays) and shouted their verses aloud, on 'the sand built ridge of heapèd hills that mound the sea . . .', 'sharing their triumph with the winds and the waves.' As the Preface somewhat portentously stated: 'We have passed the Rubicon and we leave the rest to fate.'

One of the maids at Somersby, in old age

The Tennyson children were, in effect, bilingual, both in the Lincolnshire patois, and in purer English; the former they learned mostly from the servants at Somersby. To the end of his days, Alfred spoke with a broad Lincolnshire accent, and could write and speak in dialect. He once remarked: 'The purest English is talked in South Lincolnshire. The dialect begins at Spilsby in Mid Lincolnshire, and that is the dialect of my Lincolnshire poems.' The old lady seen here remembered Alfred, whom she looked after in his early years: 'I could have liked to have heard Mr. Halfred's voice again; such a voice it was. . . .' She recalled 'how fond Mr. Halfred was of going to see the poor people and how he would often read to them, from cottage to cottage. . . .'

Charles Clarke, the schoolmaster at Somersby, about 1860

The three eldest Tennyson boys attended the tiny village school in Holywell Wood held in a ramshackle building. once the village bath house, behind the rectory. Over the door was written the text: 'Remember Now Thy Creator'. Shortly after they left for the hated Grammar School at Louth, the school was closed by the local squire who claimed that the children were disturbing his game birds.

27

POEMS,

BY TWO BROTHERS.

" HÆC NOS NOVIMUS ESSE NIHIL."---*Martial.*

LONDON:

PRINTED FOR W. SIMPKIN AND R. MARSHALL,

STATIONERS'-HALL-COURT;

AND J. AND J. JACKSON, LOUTH.

MDCCCXXVII.

above
Louth Market Place, about 1848
T. W. Wallis

In the centre of the picture is the printing office of Jacksons who, with commendable courage, agreed to the risky undertaking of publishing *Poems by Two Brothers*, in 1827.

left
Poems by Two Brothers
Less than half were by Charles. Frederick also contributed four of the poems; in later years Alfred dismissed those he wrote as 'early rot'. Certainly, they are more remarkable for the breadth of reading and reference that lay behind them than poetic originality, and some other of his early poems are much more powerful.

right
Alfred Tennyson, about 1829
Anne Weld: copy in pencil from a daguerreotype

This is the earliest known portrait of Tennyson, made by his sister-in-law. Tantalisingly, the original daguerreotype has disappeared. Another version shows him as a less handsome youth, with a bony nose and greasy, straggling hair. Since it is by someone outside the immediate family circle, it may be closer to the truth. But it is noticeable that Alfred, all through his life, had a mercurial quality, which made photographs of him, although taken only days apart, portray a quite different character.

A. Weld

I N AUGUST 1820, old George Tennyson received a letter from his eldest son that expressed the feelings of slight and injury which had been growing over two decades, ever since, indeed, the Old Man's preference for Charles had been made manifest. The control and dignity of the letter cannot disguise the anguish which lies behind it. From this point Dr Tennyson's health declined; and life for his wife and children began to assume that dismal quality which his son Arthur expressed in his drawing of 'Brothers in Misery.' The Doctor's accusation was unambiguous:

With the sentiments you yet entertain and have entertained for more than twenty years, I cannot wonder you told Mr. Bourne you had not a spark of affection for me. The rude and unprecedented manner in which you first addressed me at Hainton, after a long absence, on your return from York (I quote your own words, 'Now you great awkward booby are you here') holding me up to utter derision . . . and your language and conduct in innumerable other instances, many of which have made a deep impression upon my mind, sufficiently prove the truth of your own assertion. You have long injured me by your suspicions. I cannot avoid them for the fault is not mine. God judge between you and me. You make and have always made a false estimate of me in every respect. You look and have always looked upon me with a jaundiced eye, and deeply and *experimentally* feeling this, I am sure that my visiting you would not contribute to your satisfaction and at the same time would materially injure my own health and comfort. Conscious also that I am thrown into a situation unworthy my abilities and unbecoming either your fortune or my just pretensions, and resisted in my every wish to promote my own interests or that of my family by removing to a more eligible situation, unaccountably kept in the dark with respect to their future prospects, with broken health and spirits, I find myself little disposed to encounter those unprovoked and sarcastic remarks in which you are so apt to indulge yourself at my expense, remarks, which though they may be outwardly borne, are inwardly resented, and prey upon the mind—the injustice, the inhumanity and the impropriety of which every one can see but yourself, and which in your last visit were levelled against the father of a large family in the very presence of his children and that father between forty and fifty years of age'.

His statements cannot be accepted without qualification. Both his father and his brother were concerned for him, especially when his health was clearly broken; although his father was now advancing into his seventies, he exerted himself to find every practicable means to relieve the Somersby Tennysons. Even Charles was willing to leave his family and to neglect his parliamentary career, in order to accompany his brother to the Continent. Yet, because all shared the same Tennyson idiosyncrasies, neither George nor Charles was able to behave with the delicacy and warmth of feeling which might have made the Doctor's resentment less painful. Of old George Tennyson, it was rightly said 'when the course of everyday things does not go smoothly his mind is perturbed and that morbid sensibility prevails.' In short, he tried to behave justly and fairly towards his elder son, but could not entirely quell his irritation at the ill-repute which Dr Tennyson was bringing on the family name in the county and beyond.

It was also difficult to determine the real nature of the Doctor's illness. He drank increasingly heavily, and when he went with his wife for a cure in Cheltenham in the spring of 1822, he wrote to his mother: 'The doctor . . . says that a scirrus has not yet formed on my liver, but that he could not have answered for the consequences if I had not immediately come here.' Two years later, he began to have fainting spells and fits which seemed epileptic. 'I fear my powers are sensibly declining,' he wrote to his brother 'and the attacks to which I am subject must necessarily injure the intellect. I have had two in the last five days.' The thought of madness clearly terrified him, especially in an age when the treatment of insanity was so rigorous and barbarous: moreover, the famous establishment of Dr Willis, who had had charge of King George III, was in the south of the county, and it was suggested in 1827 that the Doctor might be put into his care. Drink, in excess, was his attempt at achieving oblivion and release from his fears and anxieties.

It was generally agreed that the great intellectual effort he made in educating his children was a prime cause of his illness, and he set great store by their prowess: 'I have some satisfaction,' he wrote in 1824, 'that my boys will turn out to be clever men. Phoenix like, I trust, (though I don't think myself a Phoenix) they will spring from my ashes in consequence of the exertions I have bestowed upon them.' Yet his younger children had not the brilliance of their elder brothers; and, after 1827, Frederick, Alfred and Charles became a source of anxiety. The Doctor became concerned, not without reason, that they were wasting their time, and his money, at Cambridge. By 1829 it was clear to his father and friends that the only palliative was to remove him from the strains which surrounded him at Somersby, pressures both intellectual and financial. His sister wrote to Charles:

I fear our poor dear brother is a pitiable sufferer, but I think and hope his sufferings not of a nature to destroy him prematurely . . . locomotion is the only thing I believe for spirits like ours when depressed and fixing exclusively on one subject.

The event which seems to have precipitated his decline into complete instability was Frederick's rustication from Cambridge for three terms. Although, characteristically, he supported and aided Frederick in his moment of need, he later brooded on events, and in his anxiety precipitated a series of bitter rages, fuelled by Frederick's inability to return a

soft answer. Elizabeth Tennyson described the position in a piteous letter of 27 February 1829 to her father-in-law:

I believe that you have been informed that Frederick said he would murder his Father. The words that Frederick made use of were these 'We may thank God that we do not live in a barbarous Country, or we should have murdered each other before this.' George did everything to irritate Frederick a few days ago and though Frederick said nothing disrespectful (as I can produce respectable witnesses to prove) he sent for the Constable (Mr. Baumber) and turned him out of doors. He remained with Mr. Baumber three days, he is now with my sister in Louth and is again taken into his father's favour who has allowed him a hundred pounds a year for the present. . . . George asserts that he had your authority for turning him out of doors. There is another and perhaps a stronger reason than any I have given for our separation, the impression which his conduct may produce upon the minds of his family, not to mention the perpetual use of such degrading epithets to myself and children as a husband and a Father and above all a person of his sacred profession ought particularly to avoid. A short time since he had a large knife and loaded gun in his room. The latter he took into the kitchen to try before he went to bed and was going to fire it off through the kitchen windows but was dissuaded. With the knife he said he would kill Frederick by stabbing him in the jugular vein and in the heart. I remonstrated with him at having such dangerous weapons and told him he would be killing himself—he said he should not do this but he would kill others and Frederick should be one. I do not say this to impair my poor husband in your opinion but only to convince you that in the state of mind in which he is at times it is not safe for his family to live with him. . . .

Dr Tennyson's anger now extended to her, her family, and his own children and he spurned Frederick's efforts to make his peace. Only a prolonged separation seemed to offer any hope of cure and in May 1829 he left for a long tour of the Continent, which was to last until the summer of 1830. It was a year of great significance for Alfred, freed for a time from the lowering presence of his father. He won the Chancellor's Medal for his poem 'Timbuctoo', published his *Poems, Chiefly Lyrical*, and cemented his friendship with Arthur Hallam when he visited the Tennysons at Somersby. For Dr Tennyson, likewise, freedom from the cares of home and family seemed to bring great benefits. He wrote pages of lyrical description of Italy and Switzerland, and the obsessive bitterness against his family abated. When he finally returned to Lincolnshire in the late summer of 1830, Frederick was in Italy, and Alfred in London; with these main sources of tension absent, he made an uneasy peace with his wife. She, however, had little illusion that normal life could be sustained for long:

It appears to me there is but little hope of any permanent tranquillity. I cannot but confess I have the greatest dread of what my happen. May God (as he has mercifully done hitherto) protect my

Alfred Tennyson, about 1834
Annie Dixon

This miniature shows a highly romanticised impression
of Alfred; yet it conveys something of the beauty of his
face, so much commented on by his friends and
contemporaries.

> 'The large dark eyes,' wrote Aubrey de Vere of the
> young Tennyson, 'generally dreamy but with an
> occasional glimpse of imaginative alertness, the
> dusky, almost Spanish complexion, the high built
> head, and the massive abundance of curling hair like
> the finest and blackest silk. . . .'

Trinity College, Cambridge: The Great Gate
From the album of Alfred, Lord Tennyson

33

Trinity College, Cambridge: New Court, 1889

The New Court, completed only a few years before Alfred came up to Cambridge, was where Arthur Hallam had his rooms; the meetings of 'The Apostles' were often held here.

Corpus Buildings, Trumpington Street, Cambridge, about 1890

Alfred and Charles first lodged in Rose Crescent, close to Trinity, but they soon moved into lodgings in Trumpington Street, with less noise and discomfort than in the rather foetid centre of the town.

family. You know as well as myself that when under the influence of liquor George is dreadfully violent.

How long this uncertain calm would have lasted can never be known, for at the turn of the year Dr Tennyson fell ill, not with any of his old complaints, but with a form of typhus. His illness at first was distressingly like his old symptoms; a nephew wrote:

He is sometimes perfectly sensible—at others, talks wildly and is evidently deranged for the time being. Dr. B. [Bousfield] says his disorder is depression of the Brain. My Uncle has been confined to his bed about a week, and I understand, gave way to great excess before his illness.

But by early March, he was 'free from all suffering and perfectly mild and tranquil; on 16 March 1831, he died.

The period of Dr Tennyson's decay compassed Alfred's tenth to twenty-third years; the effects on his development at so sensitive and impressionable an age are easy to imagine. As his wife was later to tell her sons: 'Many a time has your father gone out in the dark and cast himself on a grave in the little churchyard near wishing to be beneath it.'

Alfred and Charles had been sent to Cambridge to remove them from the fevered atmosphere of Somersby; it was a translation which Alfred did not welcome wholeheartedly. As he wrote to his aunt, Elizabeth Russell:

I am sitting owl-like and solitary in my rooms (nothing between me and the stars but a stratum of tiles). The hoof of the steed, the roll of the wheel, the shouts of drunken Gown and drunken Town come up from below with a sea-like murmur. . . . I know not how it is, but I feel isolated here in the midst of society. The country is so disgustingly level, the revelry of the place so monotonous, the studies of the University so uninteresting, so much matter of fact. None but dry-headed, calculating, angular little gentlemen . . .

His shyness was perhaps only to be expected from a boy who had never been to a town larger than Louth, and his straightforward guileless manner immediately marked him out. His first year was spent mostly in the company of Charles, with whom he shared lodgings, and with Frederick, who had transferred to Trinity to join his brothers; in his second year, he began to make his way independently. By the summer of 1829, he was lionised by a small circle of intelligent and discerning undergraduates, and, more important, had, for the first time, made a deep and fulfilling friendship outside his own family circle. The personality of Arthur Henry Hallam was remarked as extraordinary by his friends at Eton: William Ewart Gladstone in old age remembered his close friend at school, Arthur Hallam, dead for sixty years, as

a spirit so exceptional that everything with which he was brought into relation during his shortened passage through this world, came to be, through this contact, glorified by a touch of the ideal.

And Fanny Kemble sister of Alfred's friend John Kemble, declared in a romantic vein: 'There was a gentleness and purity almost virginal in his voice, manner and countenance . . .' Yet Hallam was no milksop; the depth of his feelings and his nervous sensibility matched that of Alfred: he too could talk darkly and write with a gloom that matched the Tennysons' of 'this incurable somnambulism of life'.

Hallam, like Alfred, was thrown unsupported into the bustle of Cambridge life. His Eton friends had gone to Oxford, and Cambridge seemed bleak: 'I am sick at heart, and chill in feeling,' he wrote in February 1829, 'and perish without something to invigorate, something to refresh.' For Alfred, to whom the whole experience of friendship outside the close confines of his family was an unknown novelty, plunged into it with the innocent wholeheartedness of an adolescent. In later years his wife Emily was to remark on his *childlike simplicity*, and his commitment to Arthur Hallam was total. The effect of their friendship was to 'invigorate' Hallam, as he desired, and to liberate Alfred from his brooding doubts. He discovered that he had a gift for friendship, and quickly gathered a coterie around him. Contact with others spurred him on; he wrote profusely, joined the Conversazione Society (The Apostles) and even, in rather Byronic fashion, espoused the cause of Revolution. And, after Arthur had visited Somersby, and fortuitously fallen in love with Alfred's sister, Emily, it seemed that he would be embraced within the family circle of the Tennysons, both friend and brother; the whole family, not merely Alfred, assumed Arthur Henry Hallam as one of their number.

For Alfred, a pure child of the Romantic Age, as for many of his contemporaries, friendship was a deep and serious matter. Friends were gained for a lifetime:

It is a mere and miserable solitude, to want true friends, without which the world is a wilderness . . . A principal fruit of friendship is the ease and discharge of the fulness and swellings of the heart, which passions of all kinds do cause and induce . . . friendship maketh indeed a fair day in the affections, from storms and tempests; but it maketh daylight in the understanding, out of darkness and confusion of thoughts . . .'

FRANCIS BACON, 'Of Friendship'

All of this was true of Alfred's relationship with Arthur Hallam. It was Hallam who pressed his claims to be a poet of genius, writing to Gladstone after Alfred's success with 'Timbuctoo': 'I consider Tennyson as promising fair to be the greatest poet of our generation, perhaps of our century.' He reviewed Alfred's *Poems, Chiefly Lyrical* (1830) in the *Englishman's Magazine*, with passion and enthusiasm. In the little more than three years that Hallam had left to live, they experienced much in common, with the expedition to Spain, the abuse hurled at *Poems, Chiefly Lyrical* by the editor of *Blackwoods Magazine*, the Doctor's illness and death, and the opposition of Hallam's father to his marriage with Emily Tennyson. The void left by Arthur Hallam's sudden and totally unexpected death at Vienna in September 1833 is unimaginable. Almost thirty years later, Tennyson said how he then 'suffered what seemed to me to shatter all my life so that I desired to die rather than to live'. In the latter part of his poem 'The Two Voices', written in the aftermath of Hallam's death, Alfred expressed the sensations which welled up in him:

> 'Heavens open inward, chasms yawn,
> Vast images in glimmering dawn,
> Half shown, are broken and withdrawn.'

37

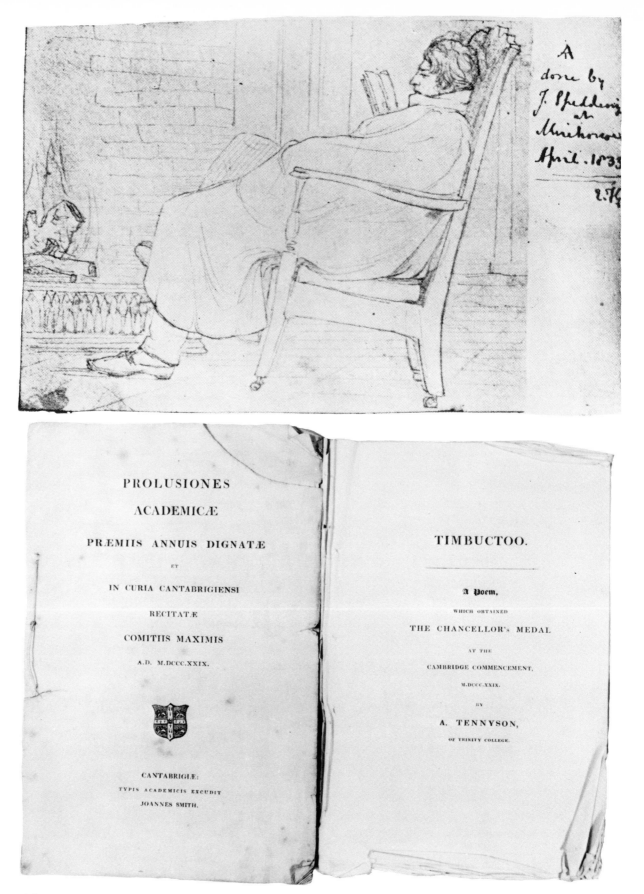

done by
J. Spedding
at Mirehouse
April. 1833
L. K.

PROLUSIONES

ACADEMICÆ

PRÆMIIS ANNUIS DIGNATÆ

ET

IN CURIA CANTABRIGIENSI

RECITATÆ

COMITIIS MAXIMIS

A.D. M.DCCC.XXIX.

CANTABRIGIÆ:

TYPIS ACADEMICIS EXCUDIT

JOANNES SMITH.

TIMBUCTOO.

A Poem,

WHICH OBTAINED

THE CHANCELLOR's MEDAL

AT THE

CAMBRIDGE COMMENCEMENT,

M.DCCC.XXIX.

BY

A. TENNYSON,

OF TRINITY COLLEGE.

Alfred Tennyson, at Mirehouse, Cumberland, 1835
James Spedding

This drawing shows Alfred's extreme short-sightedness clearly. The holiday in the Lake District was achieved only at the price of selling the Chancellor's Gold Medal, which he had won for 'Timbuctoo', so as to pay for the the trip. In the Speddings' house at Mirehouse, he found the rest and majestic scenery he needed to restore his spirits. Spedding, always a friend to him, felt that the three months removed from Somersby had been successful: 'I think Alfred took in more pleasure and inspiration than anyone could have supposed who did not know his almost personal dislike of the present, whatever it may be.' In the Lakes, he also met Edward Fitzgerald, and formed the basis of a lifelong friendship, Fitzgerald's approval was unconditional: 'I will say no more of Tennyson than that the more I have seen of him, the more cause I have to think him great. His little humours and grumpiness were so droll that I was always laughing.'

Timbuctoo
Published in 1829, here printed in *Prolusiones Academicae*

Alfred Tennyson's winning poem on the set theme of Timbuctoo was an extended version of an earlier poem, 'Armageddon'. Indeed, Dr Tennyson pressed him to enter, and Alfred was amazed to win, a surprise shared by most of those around him. He preferred Hallam's entry on the same theme. Tennyson never printed the poem in any collection of his work, and seemed a little embarrassed by his success. When the poem was to be included in a reprint of Cambridge prize poems, he wrote: 'I could have wished that poor *Timbuctoo* might have been suffered to slide quietly off, with all its errors, into forgetfulness.'

Arthur Henry Hallam (1811–32), about 1832
James Spedding

Arthur was the eldest son of the noted historian Henry Hallam. At Eton (1822–7) he wrote both prose and poetry with great fluency and assurance. Born into elevated Whig circles, he was clearly destined to succeed. Before he went to Cambridge, he had mastered French and Italian, and had read Dante, Petrarch, and the French classic authors in the original. The whole circle at Cambridge wrote verse to each other; Alfred's lines to him are an expression of their friendship:

So, friend, when first I looked upon your face
Our thought gave answer, each to each, so true
Opposèd mirrors each reflecting each—
That though I knew not in what time or place,
Methought that I had often met with you,
And either lived in either's heart and speech.

The 'Spanish Adventure', 1830. Arthur
Hallam reading one of Scott's novels to Alfred
Tennyson, Robertson Glasgow, and the
Harden family, on shipboard
John Harden

The government of Ferdinand VII in Spain was
notorious for its oppression, and through John Sterling,
the mainstay of the Apostles, Tennyson and his friends
became involved in an attempt to depose him, led by
General Torrijos. It was the Romantic idealism of
Alfred's poem, 'During the Convulsions in Spain',
translated into action:

Roused is thy spirit now
Spain of the lofty brow. . . .
Sweetly may freedom's rays
Smile on thy future days
Smile on the hopes of the young and brave . . .

Arthur and Alfred were in no danger, and after some
weeks in the Pyrenees, they returned home, with Alfred
exhilarated by the power and beauty of the mountains.
The outcome was harsher for Sterling's cousin, Robert
Boyd, who had sailed with the main party to Gibraltar.
Caught by the Spanish authorities, he died with his
companions, who were executed by a military firing
squad on the esplanade at Malaga.

For the other Tennysons too, Hallam symbolised a new beginning, free from the anguish
of their father's last years. Frederick spoke for them all when he wrote in December 1833:

We all looked forward to his society and support through life in sorrow and in joy, with the fondest
hopes, for never was there a human being better calculated to sympathize with and make
allowance for those peculiarities of temperament and those failings to which we are liable.

Not until the publication of *In Memoriam A.H.H.* in 1850, and Alfred's marriage to Emily
Sellwood, whom he had first met in 1830, while she was walking with Arthur Hallam in
the wood behind Somersby, was the pain of Hallam's death assuaged, and transmuted
into a positive force.

40

THE EMOTIONAL crosscurrents of Alfred's life in the years following the death of Arthur Hallam found reflection in the lines published in 1837:

Oh! that 'twere possible
After long grief and pain
To find the arms of my true love
Round me once again

When I was wont to meet her
In the silent woody places
By the home that gave me birth
We stood tranced in long embraces
Mixt with kisses sweeter sweeter
Than anything on earth

A shadow flits before me,
Not thou but like to thee;
Ah Christ, that it were possible
For one short hour to see
The souls we loved, that they might tell us
What and where they be . . .

The frustration and despair they express were at variance with his outward behaviour and attitudes. He produced some fine work at this time, notably 'Ulysses' and 'St. Simeon Stylites' and he seemed, unlike his sister Emily, to throw off the gloom induced by Hallam's death with surprising ease. He showed more than passing interest in Sophie Rawnsley, daughter of his father's friend, the Rector of Halton Holgate; more important, Alfred conceived a passion for Rosa Baring, a rich heiress who had been living at Harrington Hall, not two miles from Somersby, since 1825. The intensity of his feelings, and the dark passions which were then roused, found expression in his later work, although he was never to talk at any length of this period in his life.

In his maturity, Tennyson fervently denied any direct biographical content to his work, save in a most general sense. Even in *In Memoriam*, he wrote, 'It must be remembered, that this is a poem, *not* an actual biography. . . . It was meant to be a king of *Divina Commedia*, ending with happiness. . . . "I" is not always the author speaking of himself, but the voice of the human race speaking through him.' Yet of all his poems, the one undoubtedly closest to him was the most autobiographical, *Maud*, published in 1855, and incorporating the lines 'O that twere possible'. His passion for it was remarkable. 'You must always stand up

above

Charlotte Rose Baring (*c.* 1813–98)
R. Buckner

The daughter of William Baring, who had made a fortune in India (his father was chairman of the East India Company), and a member of an eminent banking family, 'Rosa' Baring was socially and financially far removed from Alfred Tennyson. In 1838 she married Robert Duncombe Shafto, a member of a rich and powerful Durham family, first cousins to her stepfather (William Baring was drowned in 1820) as well as close friends to the Russells, the family into which Alfred's Aunt Elizabeth had married. The profusion of the 'rose' imagery in Tennyson's poetry is an echo of Rosa, and in *The Roses on the Terrace* (which he probably wrote in 1889 when he heard of Robert Shafto's death) is a deep affection, long after he had last seen her:

Rose, on this terrace fifty years ago,
When I was in my June, you in your May,
Two words, '*My* Rose' set all your face aglow,
And now that I am white and you are grey,
That blush of fifty years ago, my dear,
Blooms in the Past, but close to me today
As this red rose, which on our terrace here
Glows in the blue of fifty miles away.

right

Harrington Hall, seen from the 'High Hall garden'
J. M. Gibson

Harrington Hall, which lies some two miles east of Somersby, was built on the foundations of a mediaeval house. The central tower is Tudor, but the rest of the house was much altered in the 1680s. The house remains much as it was in the days Alfred lived at Somersby, and it was the beauty of the house and its setting which inspired *Maud* as much as Rosa Baring herself. The gardens were 'formalised' in the later nineteenth century, but they have now been restored to a more natural state, 'a garden of roses/And lilies fair on a lawn'.

for Maud when you hear my pet bantling abused,' he told his friends, the Bradleys; Jane Walsh Carlyle noted that Alfred was 'strangely excited about *Maud* . . . as sensitive to criticisms as if they were imputations upon his honour.' The poem, replete, as one angry critic wrote, with 'adultery, fornication, murder and suicide', prompted savage reactions. One letter to him began: 'Sir, once I worshipped you, now I loathe you', and closed: 'you BEAST!' But all his denials could not conceal his involvement in the subject matter of the poem, as his son Hallam wrote:

There was peculiar freshness and passion in his reading of Maud, giving the impression that he

Bayons Manor, about 1890

Bayons Manor, before rebuilding, about 1820

Old George Tennyson rebuffed all the efforts of his younger son to persuade him to adopt the more noble name of d'Eyncourt, or to rebuild the old manor house into something more in keeping with his aspirations. However Charles did make his father insert a provision in his will that he should assume the name d'Eyncourt as a condition of inheriting his estate at Usselby; this was a common practice. But George Tennyson was insistent that the old house should be preserved, and when the house was rebuilt the old manor was simply absorbed within the new structure.

had just written the poem, and that the emotion it created was fresh in him. This had an extraordinary influence upon the listener who felt that the reader had been *present* at the scenes he described, and that he still felt their bliss or agony.

Indeed, in this poem and elswhere lie the bare bones of his last years at Somersby.

When Alfred became attached to Rosa Baring, he soon realised that the small sum which had come to him on his grandfather's death in 1835 was quite insufficient to support his wife; his penury was harder to bear with his uncle's largesse flowing forth upon a house and immediate family not thirty miles away. The power of wealth to distort the paths of human happiness becomes a repeated theme in his work. In *Maud* the allusions to his own circumstances are thinly disguised. The heritage of madness, with his brother Edward in mind, together with his father's derangement, his grandfather's concern for wealth and position and his uncle's vainglory, all find echoes in the poem. Much of his grandfather is found in the lines:

> But that old man, now lord of the broad estate and the Hall,
> Dropt gorged from a scheme that left us flaccid and drain'd . . .

46

Bayons Manor, a fanciful impression from the park, about 1848

The new house was a veritable pageant of English mediaevalism. It was built of elements dating, in style, from Early Norman to the fifteenth century. It was decorated with specially commissioned statues of English kings, fanciful representations of ancestors, and the blazoned arms of the d'Eyncourts, Lovels, Beaumonts, Marmions, Greys, Plantagenets, and others, from whom Charles Tennyson d'Eyncourt claimed descent. The whole area encompassed by the moat and walls was some six and a half acres.

He caricatured the rising towers of the new Bayons, and his Uncle Charles, who had now added the name D'Eyncourt to Tennyson in 1835

> Seeing his geegaw castle shine
> New as his title, built last year . . .

But it is the impersonal corruption of money, Mammon, which he most powerfully condemns, in *Maud* and in other poems. Maud's home is rendered impure by the taint of money:

> There are workmen up at the Hall: they are coming back from abroad:
> The dark old place will be gilt by the touch of a millionaire.

So too is she wooed by a man whose grandfather had been

> Master of half a servile shire
> And left his coal all turned to gold . . .

47

And the fate of one who marries for money and position, not love, is made brutally clear in 'Locksley Hall':

> Yet it shall be; thou shalt lower to his level day by day
> What is fine within thee growing coarse to sympathise with clay.
>
> As the husband is, the wife is: thou art mated with a clown,
> And the grossness of his nature will have weight to drag thee down
>
> He will hold thee, when his passion shall have spent its novel force
> Something better than his dog, a little dearer than his horse.

The anger of his curse has all the vibrant hatred of Alfred for the empty conventions and constraints which embroiled him:

> Cursed be the social wants that sin against the strength of youth!
> Cursed be the social lies that warp us from the living truth!
>
> Cursed be the sickly forms that err from honest Nature's rule!
> Cursed be the gold that gilds the straitened forehead of the fool!

He was seeking a unity; friendship of the pattern he had experienced with Hallam, but in a wife who would embody these qualities. It became clear to him that it could not be Rosa (Faultily faultless, icily regular, splendidly null/Dead perfection) although, at the end of his life, he wrote a poem which united memories of the 'High Hall Garden' with his life at Aldworth, and he remembered her with affection. But he was seeking a 'wondrous creature', someone who would be 'lovely all her life long in comeliness of heart'. He met such a paragon in Emily Sellwood, of Horncastle.

right
The baronial Great Hall of Bayons Manor, 1851

Built in the style of the late fourteenth century, it was the scene of a great banquet at which Charles's favourite son presented his father with a fine chalice, before a huge crowd of retainers, hangers-on, and the worthies of the county. Yet despite his efforts to be seen as a great magnate, he was mocked within the county and beyond.

THE EVENTUAL departure of the Tennyson family from the rectory to which Elizabeth Tennyson had come almost thirty years before, was almost as significant a landmark as the death of the Doctor. In the years following his demise their sense of resentment and inferiority had grown. They were dependent on the charity of the Old Man of the Wolds (since their only income had come from Dr Tennyson's parishes), and when he died in 1835, he was found to have made provision for them in his will. But it was on a meagre scale, and their poverty seemed all the more oppressive by contrast with the flamboyant extravagance of Uncle Charles as he began to rebuild Bayons. In 1837, the incumbent of Somersby required the rectory for his own use and the Somersby Tennysons were forced to look for a new home. Sergeant Arabin, the husband of a friend of Mrs Tennyson's, possessed an estate some fifteen miles from London in Epping Forest, and he offered them an attractive house in a small park. High Beech, as its name indicated, stood on a wooded ridge above Waltham Abbey, then still rural despite its proximity to London. The family was reduced in number, for Frederick had taken his legacy and returned to Italy, which he loved, Edward, by now clearly insane, was in an asylum, and Charles married to Louisa Sellwood, the sister of Alfred's future wife. Alfred continued in the position he had assumed at his father's death as head of the family. He organised the move, and the equipment of the new house, with impressive efficiency.

The departure from Somersby, and a sense of dislocation from his roots, was perhaps more profound for him than for his siblings: 'Dim mystic sympathies with tree and hill reaching far back into childhood,' he wrote to Emily Sellwood. 'A known landskip is to me an old friend that continually talks to me of my own youth and half forgotten things, and, indeed, does more for me than many an old friend that I know.' Yet the advantages of Epping rather than Somersby were considerable: Alfred was enabled both to see his Cambridge friends, and make many new acquaintances, and he was also drawn into the London literary world. Through James Spedding, Edward Fitzgerald and John Sterling (who had promoted the 'Spanish adventure' at Cambridge), he became known to the established *literati* of London; by 1842 he counted the veteran poet Samuel Rogers, William Makepeace Thackeray, Thomas and Jane Walsh Carlyle, the actor-manager W. C. Macready, as well as the poet Aubrey de Vere, among his admirers. Carlyle wrote a vivid description of Alfred at this time in a letter to Ralph Waldo Emerson in the United States:

A great shock of rough dusky hair, bright, laughing, hazel eyes, massive aquiline face, most massive yet most delicate, of sallow brown complexion, almost Indian looking, clothes cynically loose, free-and-easy, smokes infinite tobacco. His voice is musical, metallic, fit for loud laughter and piercing wail, and all that may lie between; speech and speculation free and plenteous; I do not meet in these late decades such company over a pipe! we shall see what he will grow to.

He was to need the support of all his friends in the difficult years which followed the family's move to Tunbridge Wells, and thence to Boxley in Kent (1840–1). Alfred's renewed acquaintance in 1836 with Emily Sellwood, whom he had first met with Arthur Hallam at Somersby and now her sister's bridesmaid, quickly blossomed into love:

> I loved thee for the tear thou could'st not hide,
> And prest thy hand, and knew the press return'd,
> And thought, 'My life is sick of single sleep:
> O happy bridesmaid, make a happy bride!'

By 1838, their engagement was an accepted fact but there seemed little prospect of marriage, with Alfred existing on the small income from his inheritance. In 1840, morbid fears on Alfred's part began to surface, and Henry Sellwood, Emily's father, a respected lawyer in Horncastle, had grave doubts about the match. Contact between them was broken off, not to be resumed for almost ten years; Emily, in middle age, was to tell her sons: 'It may have been a mistake. It was done from good motives but caused many miseries.'

His poems published in 1842 had a mixed reception, although his friends loyally applauded. Rogers wrote to him: 'few things, if any, have ever thrilled me so much', and Charles Dickens, likewise responding supportively, wrote, 'to the man whose writings enlist my whole heart and nature in admiration of their truth and beauty'. But private letters could not blot out public criticism, especially in so sensitive a nature as Alfred's, and his general state of morbidity made it all the more difficult to face the financial catastrophe that broke upon him. Early in 1841 he had been charmed into investing his whole capital in a speculative venture for wood carving by machinery. Two years later, when the scheme crumbled, with the loss of all the money invested, Alfred's despair was absolute: 'I have drunk one of the most bitter draughts out of the cup of life which go near to make men hate the world they move in.' Insanity and pain seemed to close around him: Septimus was ruled by an inertia all too reminiscent of Edward's insanity, while Arthur, like his father, had succumbed to drink. Charles's marriage had broken, a victim to his addictive need for opiates; his wife Louisa's mind shattered under the strain. The only support of any substance which Alfred could find in this extremity was the warmth and practicality of his old friend Edmund Lushington, who had married Cecilia, his favourite sister, in 1842; but when Alfred wrote to Fitzgerald in the New Year of 1844, from a sanatorium (in Cheltenham, whence the Tennysons had moved late in 1843), there was no doubt of the depths to which he had sunk:

It is very kind of you to think of such a poor forlorn body as myself. The perpetual panic and horror of the last two years has steeped my nerves in poison: now I am left a beggar but I am or shall be shortly somewhat better off in nerves. I am in an Hydropathy Establishment near Cheltenham (the only one in England conducted on pure Priessnitzan principles). I have had four crisises (one larger than had been seen for two or three years in Grafenberg—indeed I believe the largest but one that has been seen). Much poison has come out of me, which no physic ever would have brought to light. Albert Priessnitz (the nephew of the great man) officiates at this establishment, and very quick and clever he is and gives me hopes of a cure in March: I have been here already upwards of two months: of all the uncomfortable ways of living sure an hydropathical is the worst: no reading by candlelight, no going near a fire, no tea, no coffee, perpetual wet sheet and cold bath and alternation from hot to cold: however I have much faith in it—

My dear Fitz, my nerves were so bad six weeks ago that I could not have written this and to have to write a letter on that accursed business threw me into a kind of convulsion. I went through Hell.

Although the icy discomforts of the water cure and, even more important, the enforced tranquillity, produced a temporary recovery, he remained as he had written half in jest to Richard Monckton Milnes: 'a nervous morbidly-irritable man, down in the world, stark-spoiled with the staggers of a mismanaged imagination, and quite opprest by fortune . . . .' His friends helped him on the practical, financial, level. Edmund Lushington had insured the life of Dr Allen the originator of the wood-carving scheme, in Alfred's favour, and when Allen died in 1845, Alfred recovered much of his lost investment. More important was the pension granted for life in the same year by Queen Victoria on the advice of Sir Robert Peel, who had formed 'a high estimate of his powers'. The matter was arranged by Arthur Hallam's father, Henry, with the help of many of Alfred's friends, notably Rogers and Brookfield. Furthermore, the success of *The Princess*, published in 1847, brought him a small but steady income. Yet he remained miserable and dissatisfied, seeking solace in travel, the very specific which had been recommended for his father in his last years. Twice more he fell so far into morbidity and a hypochondriacal peevishness that he again

52

Thomas Woolner (1826–92)

A prominent member of the Pre-Raphaelite
Brotherhood, he produced a number of busts and
medals of Tennyson at different periods in his life, the
earliest, a medal, in 1850. In later years, he was a
regular visitor to Farringford, and one of the small band
of companions who used to go on holiday with him. It
was Woolner who suggested the subjects for Alfred's
poems, *Enoch Arden* and *Aylmer's Field*, and he was a
profound admirer of his work from their early meetings
in London in the 1840s.

essayed the 'water cure'. Carlyle writing to Emerson was certain that he had reached to
the root of the problem:

I like him well, but can do next to nothing for him. Milnes, with general co-operation, got him a
Pension; and he has bread and tobacco: but that is a poor outfit for such a soul. He wants a *task*;
and, alas, that of spinning rhymes, and naming it 'Art' and 'high Art' in a Time like ours, will
never furnish him.

But the difficulty was deeper and more personal. To Aubrey de Vere, he once said that 'he
could not longer bear to be knocked about the world, and that he must marry and find love
and peace, or die . . . .' Although he had only met Emily Sellwood once since their
engagement ended in 1840, and on that occasion by accident, there is no doubt that he
had her constantly in mind. He proposed to her in 1848, only to be rebuffed, on the
grounds that they 'moved in worlds of religious thought so different that the two would
not "make one music" as they moved . . .'; she was later to remark to Aubrey de Vere
'her great and constant desire is to make her husband more religious, or at least conduce,
as far as she may, to his growth in the spiritual life.' Only the sight of the untitled 'Elegies',
later to be published as *In Memoriam A.H.H.*, the title they both favoured, revealed his real
religious depths to her. In returning to Alfred the copy lent to her by her cousin Catherine
Rawnsley, Emily wrote, in a note which she 'was almost afraid to send': 'I have read the
poems through and through and through and to me they were and they are ever more a
spirit monument grand and beautiful, in whose presence I feel admiration and delight, not
unmixed with awe . . . .' The letter was written on 1 April 1850; on the thirteenth of June,
Alfred and Emily were married.

Stephen Spring-Rice (1814–65), 1865
O. G. Rejlander

Born into a noble Welsh family, a son of Lord Dynevor, Stephen Spring-Rice was a friend of Alfred's at Cambridge; one of his sisters married Henry Taylor, another Cambridge contemporary, and Mary Spring-Rice married James Marshall, of Tent Lodge, Coniston, where the Tennysons spent their honeymoon. In poor health, he died relatively young, to the regret of both Alfred and Emily: 'No new friends can be like the old,' she wrote to Aubrey de Vere.

W. H. Brookfield (1809–74), about 1865
Julia Margaret Cameron

'Your Early Friend' is the inscription on this photograph; Brookfield, like Henry Taylor, married within 'the Cambridge circle'. His wife, Jane Elton, was Arthur Hallam's cousin, and together they helped and supported Alfred, especially in the years before his marriage. Brookfield became a successful London clergyman and a fashionable preacher, but he never lost the bubbling sense of humour which made him dear to his friends at Cambridge. As one of them wrote in later years, 'He was by far the most amusing man I ever met, or shall meet. At my age it is not likely that I shall ever again see a whole party lying on the floor for the purposes of unrestrained laughter, while one of their number is pouring forth, with a perfectly grave face, a succession of imaginary dialogues, between characters real and fictitious, one exceeding another in humour and drollery.'

James Spedding (*left*) (1808–81) and F. D. Maurice (1805–72), about 1859
O. G. Rejlander

James Spedding shaped both Tennyson's life and his work. Through him, he kept up with his old friends and made new acquaintances: Spedding had a generous spirit and a gift for friendship. He went to school with Edward Fitzgerald, his father was a friend of Henry Taylor's family; his rooms in Lincoln's Inn Fields were almost a lodging house for Alfred and his other friends. Through Henry Taylor he found work at the Colonial Office, which at least provided a steady income, although he discovered that Downing Street was 'no place for the indulgence of individual genius'. But his scholarly claim to fame was his work on Lord Bacon, which Carlyle, who had great affection for him, described as 'the hugest and faithfullest piece of literary navvy-work I have met with in this generation . . . There is a grim strength in Spedding, quietly, very quietly invincible, which I did not know of till this book.' But in personality there was nothing grim about Spedding. For Alfred he provided a refreshing vivacity. and sound critical sense; it was Alfred he asked for by name during his last illness.

Frederick Denison Maurice, although he had left Cambridge by the time Alfred arrived at Trinity, remained a powerful influence there. With John Sterling, he had established the Conversazione Society (The Apostles), and set an elevated intellectual tone. Although a Dissenter by origin, he took orders in the Church of England, and in 1840 was appointed Professor of Literature at King's College London; in 1846, he added the professorship of Theology to his quiver. A man of ferociously independent mind, he outraged conventional opinion with his *Theological Essays* (1853) and was expelled from his Chair of Theology. Alfred cherished him, as he showed by asking him to be the infant Hallam's godfather, and rose to attack his critics in his poem 'To the Rev. F. D. Maurice':

Come when no graver cares employ
Godfather, come and see your boy:
Your presence will be sun in winter,
Making the little one leap for joy....

Should all our churchmen foam in spite
At you, so careful of the right,
Yet one lay-hearth would give you welcome
(Take it and come) to the Isle of Wight;

Thomas Carlyle (1785–1881)

'About poetry and art Carlyle knew nothing', Alfred once said, 'I would never have taken his word about either; but as an honest man, yes, —on any subject in the world.' Alfred first met the Carlyles in London, and thereafter became almost a fixture at the Carlyles' house in Cheyne Walk. By the time Alfred met him, he was already a great figure, and fast becoming a sage, far removed from the stonemason's cottage in Ecclefechan, Dumfriesshire, where he was born. Of all Alfred's friends he matched him most closely, both in the waywardness of his character, and rather rough, uncut quality. Queen Victoria described him in 1869 as: 'A strange-looking eccentric old Scotchman, who holds forth in a drawling melancholy voice, with a broad Scotch accent, upon Scotland and the utter degeneration of everything. . . .'

Jane Welsh Carlyle (1801–66)

Alfred was a little alarmed by Jane Welsh Carlyle, a woman of fiercesome intellect, mordant tongue, and considerable wit; 'Mr. and Mrs. Carlyle on the whole enjoyed life together, else they would not have chaffed one another so heartily', he once told his son.
On the other hand, Margot Tennant, the future Margot Asquith, remembered an occasion when they discussed the matter in 1889:

MARGOT: 'It seems a pity that they ever married; with anyone but each other, they might have been perfectly happy.'
TENNYSON: 'I totally disagree with you. By any other arrangement four people would have been unhappy instead of two. . . .'

56

right
W. C. Macready (1793–1873)

Alfred met the Carlyles through John Sterling and,
through him, also William Charles Macready, one of the
most successful actor managers of the day. He took his
farewell of the stage at Drury Lane, and Alfred wrote a
poem for the occasion, as a token of his friendship and
affection:

Farewell, Macready, since this night we part,
Go, take thine honours home; rank with the best,
Garrick and statelier Kemble, and the rest
Who made a nation purer through their art.
Thine is it that our drama did not die,
Nor flicker down to brainless pantomime,
And those gilt gauds men-children swarm to see...

Coventry Patmore (1823–96)

The man who rescued the 'butcher's book' in which *In Memoriam* was written, forgotten by Tennyson in the larder of his lodgings, Patmore first met Alfred in 1845, and idolised him. He, like Tennyson, had a most irregular childhood; in the same way, his marriage, three years before Alfred's was of great importance to his success. *The Angel in the House*, published in 1854, celebrated marriage, and became an epitome of Victorian social morality. It was on the death of Patmore's wife in 1862 that the relationship of deep friendship was fractured, for reasons that are not entirely clear. But Patmore could be 'haughty, imperious, combative, sardonic. . . .' and took offence at an act of kindness which Alfred rather clumsily accomplished. Thereafter, they had no more contact, despite the efforts of Thomas Woolner to bring them together; even after Patmore came to live only ten miles from Farringford in 1891, neither made any attempt to meet.

William Allingham (1824–89)

Born in Donegal, Allingham served in the Irish Customs Service and like Coventry Patmore, who provided him with an introduction, he reverenced Tennyson. He was invited to Chapel House for the first time in 1851, where he was 'shown upstairs into a room with books lying about', where he met Tennyson for the first time. Thereafter, Allingham's diary records his meetings with 'The Great Man' in tireless detail, something of a *Boswell* to Tennyson's *Johnson*. In 1874 he married Helen Paterson, a noted book illustrator and water colourist, and to her we owe a fine set of water colour impressions of Farringford and Aldworth, as well as numerous other sketches of the Tennysons at home. Like so many of Alfred's friends, Allingham died before him, and he was struck by his last words, redolent of Irish mysticism: 'I can see such things as you cannot dream of.'

Edward Fitzgerald (1809–83)

'Old Fitz', the translator of *The Rubáiyát of Omar Khayyám*, was at Trinity with Alfred, and from the letters with which he bombarded his friends, issued from the seclusion of his house at Woodbridge in Suffolk, his constant critic, informant, sage advisor, and warm friend. His letters to Frederick Tennyson in Italy, with whom he shared a common passion for music, to Spedding and Thackeray, and to the other members of the Cambridge circle, functioned as a post exchange for news and information. He could also be blunt, and he made no secret of his preference for Alfred's early work: 'I am considered a great heretic', he said to Hallam Tennyson in 1876, 'because like Carlyle I gave up all hopes for him after The Princess.' But their mutual affection never dimmed, even if Alfred was sometimes stung by his criticism, and Fitzgerald could be tart in his description of Tennyson in letters to other friends. The essence of their relationship is summed up in the last lines of Alfred's dedication of *Tiresias* to 'Old Fitz':

. . . in our younger London days,
You found some merit in my rhymes,
And I more pleasure in your praise.

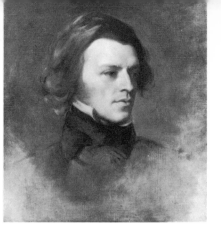

EIGHTEEN HUNDRED AND FIFTY was Alfred's *Annus Mirabilis.* He was accepted by Emily Sellwood, and in that same summer, published *In Memoriam A.H.H.*, which was to sell some 60,000 copies by the end of the year. In November, after some lobbying by his friends and admirers, including the Prince Consort, he was appointed Poet Laureate, in succession to Wordsworth.

His marriage transformed him. Aubrey de Vere recorded with delight: 'I have never before had so much pleasure in Alfred's society. He is far happier than I ever saw him before; and his "wrath against the world" is proportionately mitigated . . .' The doubts of his sister Mary, that 'I hope they will be happy, but I feel very doubtful about it . . .' were nullified by the unity and content which they showed. They spent three months in the Lake District at the home of Stephen Spring-Rice's sister, Mary Marshall. Coming south, they stayed with Edmund and Cecilia Lushington, while as Emily wrote to a friend, 'Poor Alfred has been house hunting in various directions and is sadly tired with the work.' His first discovery was a disaster. An old house at Warninglid, near Horsham, proved both remote and probably haunted, and after a few nights they left in haste, Alfred pushing the now-pregnant Emily along the rough country roads in a bath chair. Fortunately, through the intervention of Henry Taylor and his wife, their next choice was more successful. 'An old fashioned Queen Anne like house, one of those built for the Court, called Chapel House from its situation, with tall narrow windows and fittings of carved oak', was how Alfred's

60

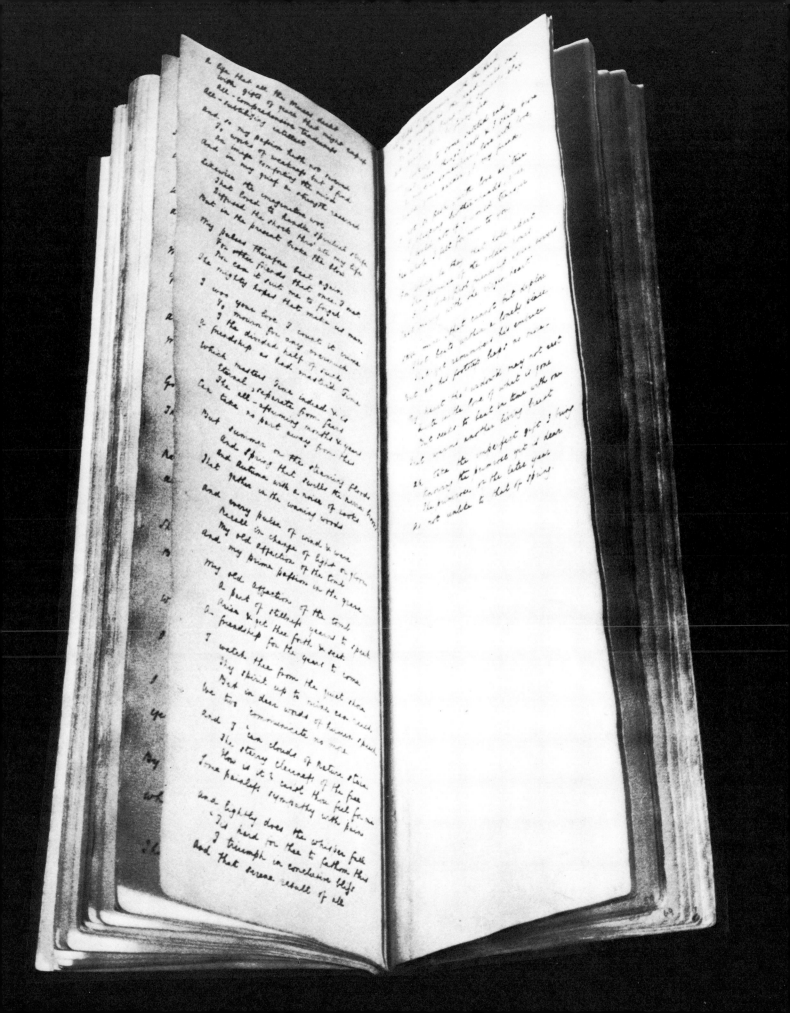

friend Francis Palgrave described the home in Montpellier Row, Twickenham, where their first (stillborn) son, and Hallam were to be born.

Although Alfred and, to a lesser degree, Emily enjoyed solitude, Chapel House experienced the regular ebb and flow of visitors which was to be repeated, on a larger scale, when they moved to Farringford in the Isle of Wight in 1853. Old friends, among them the Brookfields, Spedding, Coventry Patmore and his wife, were joined by many new connections, like Charles and Julia Cameron, Henry Taylor, and the scholar Benjamin Jowett.

Alfred Tennyson, bust by Thomas Woolner,
1857
Thomas Woolner

In November 1855 Thomas Woolner wrote to Emily Tennyson: '. . . a bust, it is what I would have wished many years, to do one of him, and I know nothing that would please me so much . . .' The result was a representation of Alfred not as he looked in 1857, as contemporary photographs make clear, but as Woolner saw him before his marriage, as a young man in London.

Marriage licence of Alfred Tennyson and Emily Sellwood, dated 15 May 1850

Alfred and Emily were married in Shiplake Church by the Vicar, Drummond Rawnsley, a friend from Lincolnshire, and the husband of Emily's cousin; it was, in Alfred's words, 'the nicest wedding' he had ever attended. In the wedding party were Emily's father, Henry Sellwood, the Lushingtons, Charles Weld (Emily's brother-in-law) and Greville Phillimore, of Shiplake House. From Shiplake, the newly married couple went to Pangbourne, and thence to Clevedon, where Arthur Hallam was buried: 'It seemed a kind of consecration to go there.' Then they went by slow stages to London via Glastonbury and Lynton, and spending some days with Alfred's mother in Cheltenham. After many offers of hospitality from friends, they decided to spend their honeymoon at Tent Lodge at Coniston, among the Lakes.

63

Chapel House, Twickenham, about 1880

The Tennysons' first son was stillborn, probably the
consequence of a fall which Emily had suffered. Alfred
was stricken by the loss. He wrote to John Forster: 'My
poor boy died in being born . . . He was a grand
massive manchild, noble brow and hands, which he had
clenched in his determination to be born . . . I kissed
his poor pale hands and came away.' Emily described
him as 'an alabaster bust of his father'.

Hallam Tennyson, at the age of nine months,
with his nurse, 1853

left

Alfred Tennyson, photographed at Tent
Lodge, Coniston, 28 September 1857,
Lewis Carroll

Charles Lutwidge Dodgson ('Lewis Carroll', 1832–98)
met Tennyson for the first time in the Lake District, and
described their first meeting: 'The door opened, and a
strange shaggy-looking man entered. He was dressed in
loosely fitting morning coat, common grey flannel

waistcoat and trousers and carelessly tied black silk
neckerchief. His manner was kind and friendly from the
first . . . there was a dry lurking-humour in his style of
talking.'

above

Hallam Tennyson, at Coniston, 28 September
1857
Lewis Carroll

67

Emily Tennyson, *née* Sellwood, 1862
G. F. Watts

Emily Tennyson's ethereal quality persisted from her early portraits, as here, through to photographs taken in her old age. 'Are you a Dryad or Oread?' was Alfred's first response on seeing her in Holywell Wood at Somersby, but this wispy, fragile impression served to mask the steel in her nature. Watts's portrait delighted both Alfred and Emily, as she wrote to him: '"This is one of the great pictures that future generations will look at" was one of the exclamations which greeted yours on its arrival. . . .' The Duke of Argyll compared it to a Gainsborough.

Lionel (*left*) and **Hallam Tennyson,** 1857
Lewis Carroll

Lionel (*left*), **Julia Marshall,** daughter of the Tennysons' hosts at Coniston, and **Hallam Tennyson,** 28 September 1857
Lewis Carroll

FARRINGFORD, THE HOUSE isolated on the western arm of the Isle of Wight, which Alfred discovered in the midst of a storm in the autumn of 1853 became for him the paradigm of a united family, the 'life within life' for which he yearned. The world which he and Emily created there for themselves and their two sons was remote from the misery and penury of Somersby; it was fitting that they were able to purchase the house, after three years as tenants, with the profits of *Maud*, which draws so much on those last years in Lincolnshire. At Twickenham they had longed for isolation, and for a sense of nature lacking within the ambit of a great city, Farringford lies at the foot of the Down, from which the chalk cliffs fell sheer to the sea below; the house possessed a wonderful solitude, so much so that when they arrived in November 1853, Emily's maids 'burst into tears saying that they could never live in such a lonely place'. The birth of their son, Lionel, so called because his father was observing the conjunction of Mars with the Lion in the sky above the house at the moment of his birth, was a confirmation of their happiness; Chapel House had always been marred by their first, stillborn, child.

Alfred's love of his children and the joy they gave him made their relationship unusually close. 'From the first,' Emily wrote, 'Alfred watched Hallam with profound interest; some of his acquaintances would have smiled to see him racing up and down stairs and dandling the baby in his arms.' His son, Hallam, when he came to write his *Memoir* of his father, remembered:

One of the very early things which I remember is that he helped the Master of Balliol to toss my brother and myself in a shawl. Later, he made us, though still very young, as much as possible his little companions. My mother was not strong enough to walk as far as we did, and so my father would harness my brother and myself to her garden carriage, and himself push from behind; and

Alfred Tennyson, photographed at Manchester, 1857
James Mudd

The Tennysons passed through Manchester on their way to the Lake District. While they were there, they heard Charles Dickens give one of his recitations of *The Christmas Carol*, and visited the National Art Exhibition held in the city. Nathaniel Hawthorne saw Alfred Tennyson there:

> The most picturesque figure without affectation that I ever saw, of middle size, rather slouching, dressed entirely in black and nothing white about him except the collar of his shirt, which methought might have been clean the day before. He had on a black wideawake hat, with round crown and wide irregular brim, beneath which came down his long black hair, looking terribly tangled; he had a long pointed beard, too, a little browner than the hair, and not so abundant as to encumber any of the expression of his face. His frock coat was buttoned across his breast though the afternoon was warm. His face was very dark, and not exactly a smooth face, but worn, and expressing great sensitiveness. . . .

70

Lear was one of the first visitors to Farringford, but his friendship with Alfred Tennyson was complicated by Lear's extraordinary prickliness and Tennyson's testiness. In June 1860, Lear recorded on a visit to Farringford: 'A.T. most disagreeably querulous and irritating . . . snubby and cross always . . . I believe that this is my last visit to Farringford,—nor can I wish it otherwise all things considered. . . .' However, his most reverential affection for Emily Tennyson always brought him back.

in this fashion we raced up hill and down dale. When the days were warm enough, perhaps we sat together on a bank in one of our home-fields, and he would read to us, or in cold weather would play football with us boys in an old chalk-pit, or build castles of flint on top of the 'Beacon Cliff,' and we all then cannonaded from a distance, or he would teach us to shoot with bow and arrow.

If it was rainy or stormy, and we were kept indoors, he often built cities for us with bricks, or played battledore and shuttlecock; sometimes he read Grimm's Fairy Stories or repeated ballads . . .

Emily, too, despite her physical fragility, loved to play with them, as she wrote to Edward Lear when Lionel was eighteen months old: 'Hallam's great delight is to ride on my back, and then Lionel must ride too, so with her two romping boys Mother has a chance of being well tired.' She was in her forty-second year when Lionel was born, and both advancing years and difficult pregnancies made it unlikely there would be more children. At Somersby, the whole tribe of brothers and sisters had provided stimulus and comfort for each other, the older children bringing up the younger; at Farringford, it was Alfred who provided companionship for his children. Towards his family, there was none of the 'Paterfamilias' in his behaviour; Emily who acted as her husband's secretary and managed

his affairs, belied the assertion of *The English Matron*, published in 1846: 'the government of a household, for the sake of all its inmates, should be a monarchy, but a limited monarchy; of all forms, a democracy is most uncomfortable in domestic life.' Alfred stood apart from the conventions of the age, following his own course and interests among his friends; he was typical of an earlier and less circumscribed age.

In 1860, Julia Margaret Cameron, whom the Tennysons already knew well from Twickenham, moved to Dimbola, close to Farringford. In 1864, she was given a camera by her daughter and son-in-law, with the message: 'It may amuse you, Mother, to try to photograph . . .' To that act we owe the unique record of the Tennysons at Farringford. The two boys possessed an 'old picture beauty', as Emily described it, which Julia Margaret Cameron exploited to the full. She also managed to inveigle Alfred, as well as many of the Tennysons' friends, staying at Farringford, to undergo the ruthless perfectionism of her portraiture. Other notable photographers recorded the 'life in life' of the Tennysons at Farringford, but perhaps only the photographer, O. G. Rejlander, caught the elusive quality which she managed to convey.

73

Farringford, 1894
F. N. Broderick

In 1871, Tennyson built the large library (with a ballroom underneath it) which was equipped with a special staircase access to enable him to escape unwelcome visitors. The books overflowed from the library into the rooms nearby, and the residue—in particular the latest novels—scattered around the house, in visitors' bedrooms, on tables and other available surfaces.

Hallam Tennyson (*left*) with his brother **Lionel,** and their tutor **Henry Graham Dakyns** (1839–1911), 1861
W. Jeffrey

Graham Dakyns became one of the closest friends of the Tennyson family. He came to Farringford in February 1861 and stayed until September 1863, then went to Clifton College as a classics master. There he formed a close friendship with John Addington Symonds, whom Benjamin Jowett sent with an introduction to the Tennysons; to Symonds we owe some interesting if somewhat overheated descriptions of Lionel and Hallam:

> But the boys . . . My heart bled and my soul yearned to them . . . there was something in the light that ran over Hallam's face, in Lionel's grace, and in the delicate fibre of both felt through their finger tips, which revealed them to me . . . I will never forget them.

Hallam and **Lionel Tennyson,** 1863
O. G. Rejlander

Symonds described Lionel as 'a splendid creature, tall and lithe, with long curls and a pear-shaped face, extremely beautiful'. He seemed 'to have come out of a chapter of past history'. Hallam was 'also mediaeval but not so handsome as his brother'.

Julia Margaret Cameron (1815–79), photographed by her brother-in-law
Lord Somers

The daughter of an eminent Anglo-Indian jurist, James Pattle, she married Charles Hay Cameron, twenty years her senior, in 1838. He retired from his legal practice in 1848, and the Cameron family settled in England. In London, they had a wide circle of friends, among them the Prinseps at Little Holland House, where Tennyson was a frequent visitor. In 1860, Julia Margaret established their home at Freshwater in a pair of converted cottages, which she named 'Dimbola' after a family estate in Ceylon (Sri Lanka), and it became the centre of the wildly eccentric household, dominated by her passion for photography after 1863. In 1875, the Camerons returned to Ceylon; shortly after a visit to England in 1878, she fell ill and died.

Julia Margaret Cameron came to photography by chance, and the extraordinary quality and power of her best work was the product of a ruthless perfectionism impossible for most commercial photographers. Her sitters endured agonies, sitting stock still for some five minutes before her enormous camera, with its massive lens of 30″ focal length. She wrote of her portrait of Tennyson's close friend, W. G. Ward: 'I counted four hundred and five hundred and got one good picture. Poor Wilfred said it was *torture* to sit long, that he was a martyr. I said that I am the martyr! Just try the taking instead of the sitting.' Her portraits, taken in a shadowy half-light in extreme close-up, penetrate the soul and nature of her sitters, as she once said: 'my whole soul had endeavoured to do its duty towards them in recording faithfully the greatness of the inner, as well as the features of the outer man.' Her narrative and life studies are less highly regarded, yet she applied the same rigorous standards in producing them; their relative disfavour is an idiocy of fashion. Many of her finest portraits triumph despite her technical imperfections, for she was never entirely master of the chemical mysteries of the craft. It was the random quality of genius which made her impossible to imitate. Others used her soft style of portraiture: none could match her results.

From life: Lionel and Hallam Tennyson, about 1861
Julia Margaret Cameron

Edith Bradley, daughter of the Tennysons' close friends, Granville and Marian Bradley, remembered Lionel and Hallam at this time as: 'straight and tall, dressed always in tunics and knee pants of the same shade of grey as their mother's gown—belted on week days, crimson-sashed and crimson-stockinged on Sundays, holidays, and everyday evenings; low strapped slippers always worn in the house, and on their broad lace collars, their long golden hair falling, Lionel's forever in his eyes . . . the younger's beauty was so great that even we children were conscious of it. He looked like his mother, whereas the elder had his father's deep-set eyes and high forehead.'

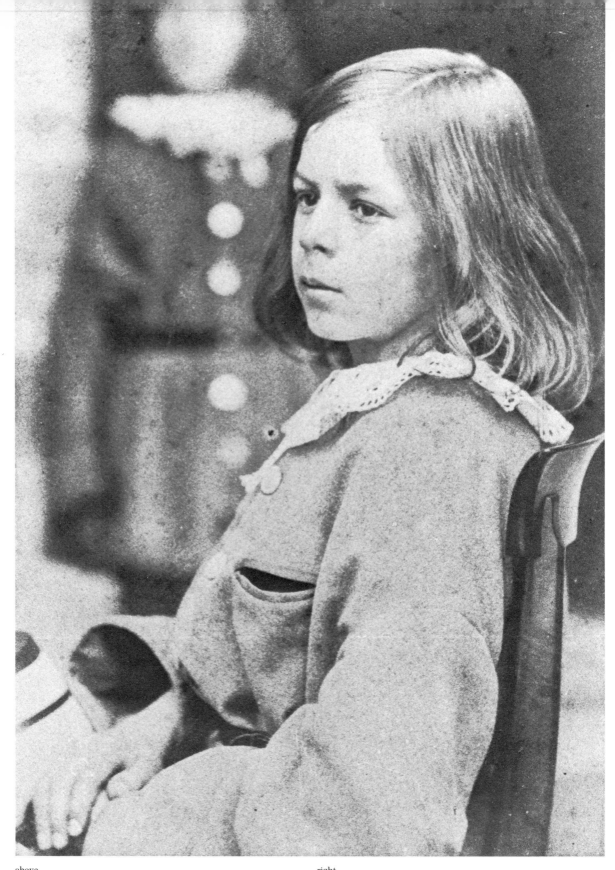

above
Hallam Tennyson, 1861
O. G. Rejlander

right
Hallam Tennyson, aged ten, 1862
I. Mayall

80

Alfred Tennyson, 1869
Julia Margaret Cameron

Alfred Tennyson, 6 May 1862
W. Jeffrey

'In came a tall, broad-shouldered swarthy man, slightly stooping with loose dark hair and beard. . . . Hollow cheeks and the dark pallor of his skin gave him an unhealthy expression . . . (William Allingham on first meeting Tennyson).

left
Emily Tennyson, with **Hallam** (*left*) and
Lionel, about 1864
W. Jeffrey

below
Alfred Tennyson, with **Hallam** (*left*) and
Lionel, about 1862
O. G. Rejlander

Generally the boys and I go into the study and read
after dinner when we are alone, but last night Ally
wished the boys to stay with him so we stayed and
they sang to him all evening. They sing some things
very sweetly together. Ally was very much charmed
with some of the singing . . . (Emily Tennyson to her
sister, Anne, and to her father).

left
Alfred Tennyson, 'The Dirty Monk', 1865
Julia Margaret Cameron

above
Emily Tennyson, about 1862
G. F. Watts

The 'Dirty Monk' portrait, as Alfred described it, and
Watts's drawing of Emily express the contrast between
his earthy energy and her frailty. Yet it was Emily's
gentle but relentless guiding spirit which ruled the
Tennyson family, including Alfred.

O. G. Rejlander (1813–75), about 1863
From the album of Lionel Tennyson

Oscar Rejlander, born in Sweden, achieved enormous renown in England as a pioneer of 'high art' photography. From his studio in Wolverhampton, established in 1855, he displayed an elaborate life-study, a composite of some thirty negatives, on the subject of *The Two Ways of Life* (Industry and Dissipation). This opulent allegory was bought by Queen Victoria, and was so much liked by the Prince Consort that he hung it in his study. Thereafter Rejlander rapidly became a fashionable photographer, much in demand, and his success was enhanced when he moved his studio to London in 1860. But he was also much attacked (the 'dissipation' section of *The Two Ways of Life* had to be discreetly shrouded when the picture was displayed in Scotland), and he wrote to a colleague 'I am tired of photography for the public, particularly composite photos, where there can be no gain and there is no honour, only cavil and misrepresentation.' However, his portraits, especially that of the Tennyson family, possess a lightness and informality lacking in his more studied work. In his later years he collaborated with Charles Darwin, providing the photographs for *The Expression of Emotions in Man and Animals.*

The Tennyson family, walking in the gardens of Farringford, May 1863
O. G. Rejlander

ALL ALFRED's brothers were afflicted by what he termed the 'black bloodedness of the Tennysons'; in Edward, this developed into an intensely nervous state. His mother recorded that: 'He weeps bitterly sometimes and says his mind is so unnotched that he is scarcely able to endure his existence.' He died in 1890 at the age of 77 in the asylum to which he had been committed in his youth. In Septimus, the dark side of his nature manifested itself in extreme inertia. Dante Gabriel Rossetti delighted in repeating his story of Septimus, whom he encountered at the Hallams' house in Wimpole Street. On being ushered into an apparently empty drawing room, he was surprised by a huge shaggy figure which rose from the hearth rug on which it had been lying full length, and advanced towards him with outstretched hand, saying, 'I am Septimus, the most morbid of the Tennysons.' His death in 1866, a year after his mother's, ended an unhappy life.

Frederick remained, as he had been since his father's death, isolated from the rest of his family. He indulged his twin passions, for Italy and music, with the income from his inheritance, and his *ménage* in Florence, which for thirteen years included his brother Arthur, was ruled with the same high-handed imperiousness which the Doctor had maintained at Somersby. In 1859, Frederick with his wife and children moved to the warmer climate of the Channel Islands, where a profound religious mysticism gradually dominated his outlook. He was converted to Swedenborgianism, as well as dabbling in spiritualism. Introspection replaced activity, and his talents were never fulfilled, as his friend Robert Browning wrote of him: 'One was always expecting them to crystallise, but they never did.'

Arthur and Horatio were gripped by the type of other-wordliness which had shown so strongly in Septimus. Edward Fitzgerald once said of Horatio that he seemed 'rather unused to the planet' and the remark could be applied equally to Arthur. Arthur, as 'idle as a foal', as his grandfather described him, was always subject to moods of black despair, and by 1842, he was drinking so heavily that he was a confirmed alcoholic. In March 1843 his mother wrote to Charles Tennyson d'Eyncourt: 'Arthur has voluntarily placed himself (to conquer the ruinous and destructive habit of drinking) in the Crichton, an institution nobly endowed for the insane and others who like to place themselves there in order to conquer any evil propensity.'

Marriage for both Horatio and Arthur was, as for Alfred, the sovereign remedy; it drew them closer to each other and to their roots in the Wolds. In 1857, Horatio married the sister-in-law of the Vicar of Wrawby, close to Grasby where Charles was Rector. Three years later, Arthur married the vicar's sister, Harriet West; thereafter, they were often to be found in Lincolnshire, startling the villagers around Grasby with their foibles and eccentricities as they had at Somersby in their youth.

Of all his brothers, Alfred was closest to Charles, and like Horatio and Arthur, they were brought closer by their marriages. Charles and his wife wrote to Alfred and Emily Sellwood on their wedding day as 'dear double sister and long-single brother'. Alone of the Tennysons, Charles felt a genuine vocation for the Church, but within months of his ordination in 1833, he was addicted to opium, 'almost killing himself with laudanum and suffering so much from lowness of spirits'; from their marriage in 1836, his wife Louisa Sellwood bore his burden with him, ruining her own health in the process. Financially, Charles, who had inherited the living of Grasby from his uncle, Sam Turner, in 1835 (and added the name Turner to his own) was well provided. He was able to act as benefactor to the primitive villagers of Grasby, still sunk in witchcraft and superstition: one of their customs when he arrived was to ward off the evil eye by cutting a sheep in half, then to put the carcass on a scarlet cloth, and walk between the pieces. Throughout his life he looked, in the words of a supercilious d'Eyncourt cousin, like 'a dogs' meat man'; one local child remembered 'his *unshaved* chin' and Louisa despaired of the way 'his surplice hung . . . about him like a clothes bag . . .'. Yet his kindness and dedication, as well as his almost excessive shyness and modesty, endeared him to his parishioners.

Alfred thought highly of his poetry, and wrote 'At Midnight, June 30, 1880' as a preface to Charles's *Collected Sonnets*, published in 1880 by Charles Kegan Paul. His reply to Gladstone, who wrote to him in appreciation of the volume, marks his true feelings about his brother, and the sense of loss he felt at his death: 'I wish indeed that you had known him: he was almost the most lovable human being I have ever met.'

Alfred Tennyson, 1864
I. Mayall

This was Tennyson's favourite portrait of himself, with
the 'Dirty Monk' running a close second.

Arthur Tennyson (1814–99) and his wife
Harriet
Arthur Tennyson

Harriet died in June 1881 and in December 1882,
Arthur married Emma Louisa Maynard. He was
devastated by Harriet's death 'walking about with one of
her gloves or handkerchiefs in his hand, and with tears
streaming down his face'.

Charles Tennyson Turner (1808–79), about 1864
I. Mayall

Frederick Tennyson (1807–98), about 1865
Julia Margaret Cameron

Horatio Tennyson (1819–99), 1867
Julia Margaret Cameron

In 1868 Horatio's first wife died and two years later he married the sister of Arthur's wife, Catherine West, which drew the brothers even closer together. During his brief period as a widower he lived in a house on the Farringford estate provided by Alfred.

Mary Tennyson (1810–84)

Mary married Alan Ker, the brother of a doctor in Cheltenham, where she was then living with her mother, brother and sisters, in 1851. A barrister, he emigrated with his wife to Jamaica to take up an opportunity in the legal service of the island. Their life was made up of many prolonged separations, and Mary found comfort in Swedenborgianism, the Church of the New Jerusalem. She succeeded in drawing both Emily and Frederick into the Church as well, and she was an ardent and active apostle for her new faith; she wrote many poems expounding her beliefs, and other less theological verse.

Emilia Tennyson (1811–87)
From the album of Lionel Tennyson

'Emily' Tennyson married Captain Richard Jesse in 1842, a man of quite different stamp from Arthur Hallam. For many years, they lived next door to her mother in Hampstead, and their marriage was a happy one. Through her sister Mary she was converted to the Church of the New Jerusalem, and remained an earnest devotee for the rest of her life. Blanche Warre Cornish wrote a succinct pen portrait of Emily in her later years: 'a deep serious voice, and she attracted me at once by her fine blue expressive eyes, which still gave forth light, though set in a deep lined face . . . She had once been Arthur Hallam's fiancée . . . [to a question] she replied with a strong Lincolnshire accent, "I know that; I have felt that." She added in a deep melodious tone, just like Horatio Tennyson's, "I have felt everything; I know everything. I don't want any new emotion. I know what it is to feel like a stoän."'

Matilda Tennyson (1816–1913)

'Tilly', never married and lived with her mother until
she died in 1865; thereafter, she spent most of her time
either with Alfred and Emily, or with her sister Cecilia at
Park House. Her nephews, Hallam and Lionel, loved her
rumbustious, tomboy quality, always willing to join in
their wild games. She was a favourite aunt. Her later
years, after Alfred's death, were spent with Cecilia in a
bizarre *ménage* at Park House, and she survived all the
rest of her family to die, cared for by her niece Zilly,
shortly before the First World War.

Cecilia Tennyson (1817–1909), 1861
Thomas Rodger

From her marriage to Alfred's Cambridge friend,
Edmund Lushington, in October 1842, Cecilia
established the one steady point in the irregular
meanderings of the Tennyson family. Park House,
Maidstone and Farringford became the two cardinal
points in the lives of the younger Tennyson brothers
and sisters. Cecilia, who found the climate of Glasgow,
where her husband was Professor of Greek, intolerable,
spent most of her time at Park House, with either the
Tennysons, or her husband's brothers, Franklin, Harry,
and Tom, as regular visitors; Henry Lushington, who
died in Malta in 1855, was especially close to Alfred.

Cecilia survived her husband by sixteen years, becoming
an ever more eccentric figure. In old age at Park House,
she was wont to cram any particularly delectable cakes
or buns set out for tea into a capacious black bag she
carried everywhere with her; when visitors were
expected, the cakes were held back until the last possible
moment, since on one occasion she had swept the whole
iced top of a large gateau into the ever-ready
receptacle.

Edmund Lushington (1811–93), 1865
Cruttenden

'O true and tried, so well and long' began the
epithalamium which Alfred Tennyson wrote for
Edmund Lushington: it was a fair statement for
Lushington provided a steadying influence, a modicum
of stability and common sense in Alfred's life. He was a
sensitive and intelligent critic of his work. The happiness
of the Lushingtons' marriage was marred by Cecilia's ill
health, and by the tragic deaths of their children. Their
only son Edmund died in 1856, aged thirteen, Emily at
the age of nineteen in 1868, and Lucia Maria in 1873;
only their second daughter Cecilia, 'Zilly', lived to
maturity, and she never married, Lushington retired as
Professor of Greek at Glasgow in 1875, and spent the
rest of his life at Park House, devoted to his wife, who
was almost broken by the deaths of her children; 'Park
House seems to be much as usual,' Emily wrote once to
Edward Lear. 'Unutterably sad.'

T HE SMALL, quaintly Gothick house at Farringford which the Tennysons purchased in 1856 remained virtually unaltered for a decade, and even when they began to enlarge the house and plant the garden, it retained the informal atmosphere of a family home. A procession of notables in the arts, Church and State passed through its doors, among them William Wilberforce, Algernon Swinburne, the Bradleys, Robert Browning, Benjamin Jowett, Charles Darwin, John Millais, the Gladstones, T. H. Huxley, Charles Kingsley and Sir John Herschel; interspersed among the dignitaries were the Tennyson brothers and sisters, close local friends like Sir John Simeon, W. G. Ward and, as their sons grew up, a host of young people. Farringford had an inner life unlike that of any other house, a quality it drew from the Tennysons themselves. Alfred's grandson, Charles Tennyson, recalled that it had an 'unforgettable charm.'

Except for the drawing-room, where enormous and slightly bowed French windows, 25 ft. across and 10 ft. in height, opened on to the glorious eastern view between a huge cedar and two great elm trees on the lawn, the rooms and passages were mysteriously dark, owing to the thick copses which pressed close to the walls and the creepers which clambered about them. Darkest of all was the dining-room. This faced north and looked straight into the heart of an immense ilex, planted in the year of Waterloo, which spread its great bulk over a grassy island in the middle of the drive. In corners and corridors glimmered masks and busts of Milton, Dante, Wordsworth, Thackeray and Tennyson himself. Dim old oil paintings bought sixty years before by Tennyson's father during his sick and solitary pilgrimages to Italy, loomed from the walls of drawing-room, dining-room and library, and the narrow staircase, with its slender balustrade of turned mahogany, was lined with dimly impressive photographs by Julia Margaret Cameron of the poet's friends, including, I remember, Sir William Herschel, Robert Browning, Thomas Carlyle, Gifford Palgrave, Charles Kingsley, F. D. Maurice and Edmund Lushington, with the strangely draped and drooping figures of the young women, mostly of the Ritchie and Prinsep families, whom Mrs. Cameron subdued so ruthlessly to her singular art.

Elsewhere there were drawings by Thackeray, Holman Hunt, Millais and Dickie Doyle, prints presented by Frederick Locker, and paintings, drawings and engravings by Edward Lear, including two of his early bird illustrations of brilliantly coloured cockatoos and, in the ballroom, a huge oil painting which he had left unfinished at his death, of a very small Enoch Arden in the middle of an enormous and luxuriant tropical island. The grim, swarthy portrait of the poet's father hung in the hall, and in the drawing room were Watts's beautiful half-length painting of my grandmother and his group of my father and my uncle, with long golden curls and curious lace-collared tunics, painted in the early 1860's before they went to school.

There were old books in sunk and wired cases, old china in cabinets, and, in the poet's great library, books up to the ceiling wherever bookcases could be fitted. Most of old Dr. Tennyson's books were there and Charles Tennyson Turner's library, and there were scores of slim volumes of contemporary verse sent by authors seeking commendation or criticism, and scores of recent and contemporary novels, many of them in three volumes, with which the poet solaced the hours when he was not in the mood for composition or study.

The furniture in the library was large, solid and austere. Tennyson wrote in a plain windsor chair facing a great bow window which looked into the darkly glimmering copse a few feet away. Beside his chair stood a curious, tall standard of spirally carved elm or pear wood in the top of which was a single candle. This can, I think, only have been used for subsidiary illumination, for he was intensely short sighted and always nervous about his eyes. The only concessions to comfort were one large upholstered arm chair by the fireside and an immense cane-bottomed day-bed, about 7 ft. long by 3 ft. wide, with crimson mattress and cushions.

On the other side of the island lies Osborne House, created by Queen Victoria and Prince Albert, to serve them as Farringford served the Tennysons, as a means of retreat from the hectic world outside. Prince Albert was the first casual visitor to Farringford after they had bought the house. Emily wrote to her sister Anne Weld on 15 May 1856:

Such a strange week as we have had. On Monday, the Monckton Milneses and Simeons to luncheon. Tuesday Prince Albert to call. Two rings at the door and Colonel Phipps or somebody announced the Prince who had come to see the fort and had heard Ally lived near and had come to ask if he would speak with them. I said I would go and fetch him and asked the Colonel to show Prince Albert into the drawing room and disappeared myself. He was very kind, shook hands with Ally and talked to him very gaily. One of his gentlemen gathered a huge bunch of cowslips which he took into his own hands and said they were so very fine (and so they are) and that they make good tea. We hear this morning he said it was a very pretty place and that he should certainly bring the Queen. It will be a pity if we miss the great honour and pleasure it would be to receive her.

The Queen never came, although Alfred with his extreme myopia once mistook the dumpy figure of Mrs Cameron for the monarch, murmuring 'Madam this is indeed an honour' as he approached. He found the Queen less daunting in audience than he had expected, even in the emotional period following the death of the Prince Consort. Queen Victoria described their meeting in April 1862:

I went down to see Tennyson who is very peculiar looking, tall, dark, with a fine head, long black flowing hair and a beard—oddly dressed, but there is no affectation about him. I told him how much I admired his glorious lines to my precious Albert and how much comfort I found in his *In Memoriam*. He was full of unbounded appreciation of my beloved Albert. When he spoke of his own loss, of that to the Nation, his eyes quite filled with tears!

His respectful and romantic attitude towards her kept them from dangerous ground. The Queen much disapproved of the visit of Garibaldi in 1864: 'The Queen much regrets the

Alfred Tennyson, about 1870
W. Jeffrey

100

Emily Tennyson, about 1870

extravagant excitement respecting Garibaldi, which shows little dignity and discrimination in the nation . . .' The Poet Laureate, by contrast, received him with delight. Emily recorded in her journal:

People on foot and on horseback and in carriages had waited at our gate two hours for him. Some rushed forward to shake hands with him. He stood up and bowed. A. and I and the boys were in the portico awaiting his arrival. On entering the house Garibaldi admired the primroses with which the rooms were decked, and liked the view of our park, and said to A., 'I wish I had your trees in Caprera.' A. and he went up to A.'s study together, and they talked on politics, A. advising the General not to talk politics in England. They repeated Italian poetry to each other.

Alfred afterwards wrote to his close friend, the Duke of Argyll:

What a noble human being! I expected to see a hero and I was not disappointed. One cannot exactly say of him what Chaucer says of the ideal knight 'As meke he was of port as is a maid'; he is more majestic than meek, and his manners have a certain divine simplicity in them, such as I have never witnessed in a native of these islands, among men at least, and they are gentler than those of most young maidens whom I know. He came here and smoked his cigar in my little room and we had a half hour's talk in English, tho' I doubt whether he understood me perfectly, and his meaning was often obscure to me.

Garibaldi, sadly, was one of the few visitors to Farringford whom Julia Margaret Cameron failed to ensnare:

Mrs. Cameron wanted to photograph Garibaldi, and dropped down on her knees before him, and held up her black hands, covered in chemicals. He evidently thought that she was a beggar until we had explained who she was.

The early days of her new-found passion corresponded with the period of 'Farringford society' at its zenith. Her single mindedness in the pursuit of her art, and the exotic chaos of her household at Dimbola, often reduced the Tennysons to helpless laughter, as Emily wrote to her father in February 1865:

I must tell you about Mrs. Cameron's 'Time.' She was talking on an interesting subject with Mr. Pollock when suddenly she rushed out with extended arms, 'Stop him! Stop him! There he is, Time.' An old man was brought in with white hair. According to Hallam, he was undressed, had no shirt on. Wanted scrubbing very much. Mrs. Cameron wraps him up in best shawls, puts an egg cup in his hand, turns him into 'Time,' but talks to him so much about his beautiful face that he is supposed to have grown very conceited at last . . .

But if her grim, dishevelled appearance, and wild enthusiasms could be ludicrous, Alfred and Emily had no doubt that her work was a wonderful creation: 'Mrs. Cameron has made some magnificent photographs, clear and smooth as well as picturesque. Ally says no Titian is so fine as that of Blumenthal. . . .' Certainly, Julia Margaret immortalised the friends whom the Tennysons entertained at Farringford, imbuing them with the timeless quality of all her portraits.

In the wake of the famous came hordes of trippers, which increased year by year, and some went to extraordinary lengths to catch a glimpse of the elusive Laureate. He inveighed endlessly against the 'Cockneys', even to the Queen, who replied, 'But we are not much troubled here by them'. Tennyson answered, 'Perhaps I should not be either Your Majesty, if I could stick a sentry at my gates.' He told Francis Palgrave, when the family had fled from the crowds to a farmhouse at Grayshott, 'I don't give the name of the place because I wish to be kept secret: I am not flying from the cockneys there to tumble in among the cockneys here. . . .' Worse than the human invasion was the steady advance of bricks and mortar. He wrote to the Duke of Argyll of his 'disgust at having Freshwater . . . so polluted and defiled . . . they talk of laying out streets and crescents and I oscillate between my desire of purchasing land at a ruinous price in order to keep my views open and my wish to fly the place altogether.' Emily wrote to an American friend, Frederick Goddard Tuckerman:

Our beautiful views will, I fear, be spoilt before long. People are seized with a building mania. Already a bit of our sea is built out from us and we are obliged to buy land at the rate of a thousand pounds an acre merely to prevent more of the bay being hidden by ugly brick houses. . . . If our down were no longer lonely we could not stay. We could only be here in the winter when it is too stormy for visitors. . . .

The other penalty of fame was more serious, for the huge volume of correspondence which Tennyson received was all handled and answered personally by Emily. In 1874, after returning from a holiday in France, she suffered a complete physical collapse, from which she recovered only slowly. Tennyson blamed the work which she had undertaken for him, knowing his distaste for writing letters, as he wrote to James Knowles:

She has overwrought herself with the multifarious correspondence of many years, and is now suffering for it. I trust that with perfect quiet she will recover; but it will never again do for her to insist upon answering every idle fellow who writes to me.

Thereafter, Emily was an invalid, and Hallam left Cambridge to take her place as his father's secretary; like Alfred before him, he never proceeded to a degree. His sacrifice was not lost on them, for as Alfred wrote to the Master of his College, Trinity, 'We are grieved that our absolute need of Hallam at home has prevented him from accomplishing his university career.' His anguish at forcing his son's life along the paths of his own convenience, echoing as it did his own youth, was unfeigned. Benjamin Jowett wrote to Hallam the day before his father died that 'he regretted that he had been a drag on you', and Alfred, weak as he was in his last days, told his son, 'I make a slave of you.' The advent of Hallam as his father's confidant marked a decisive shift in the Tennysons' lives; Alfred was now becoming an old man, dependent to an ever-increasing degree on his willing son. As his friends began to die off—his brother Charles and Julia Margaret Cameron in 1879 and Fitzgerald in 1883—he came to depend on Hallam for companionship. It was now Hallam rather than Francis Palgrave or other friends who usually accompanied him on holiday each summer, and life at Farringford began to lose some of the sparkle of earlier and more ebullient days. One visitor, Phillips Brooks, who visited the house in 1882, left a description which conveys the atmosphere, now much more formalised, of Farringford in the last decade of Tennyson's life:

. . . a pretty drive over the Downs, with two or three small villages upon the way, brought us, in about three miles, to this house. Here the great poet lives. He is finer than his pictures, a man of good six feet and over, but stooping as he walks, for he is seventy-four years old, and we shall stoop if we ever live to that age. A big dome of a head, bald on the forehead and the top, and very fine to look at. A deep bright eye, a grand eagle nose, a mouth which you cannot see, a black felt hat, and a loose tweed suit. These were what I noticed in the author of 'In Memoriam.'

The house is a delightful old rambling thing, whose geography one never learns, not elegant but very comfortable, covered with pictures inside and ivies outside, with superb ilexes and other trees about it, and lovely pieces of view over the Channel here and there.

He was just as good as he could be, and we all went to a place behind the house, where the trees leave a large circle, with beautiful grass, and tables and chairs scattered about. Here we sat down and talked. Tennyson was inclined to be misanthropic, talked about Socialism, Atheism, and another great catastrophe like the French Revolution coming on the world. . . . We had tea out of doors, took a walk for various views, then, having come to know me pretty well, he wanted to know if I smoked, and we went up to his study, a big, bright, crowded room, where he writes his Idylls, and there we stayed till dinner-time.

Drawing by William Makepeace Thackeray (1811–63) for Tennyson's *The Lord of Burleigh*; it used to hang on the study wall at Farringford

Tennyson had known Thackeray at Cambridge, and saw him frequently in London after the family moved to High Beech. Thackeray admired Tennyson, both for his poetry and for his conversation; on one occasion he burst out, 'My dear Alfred, you do talk damn well.' With his death in 1863, his two daughters were left alone, and the Tennysons welcomed them at Farringford.

The summer house at Farringford where Tennyson wrote *Enoch Arden* and did much of his other work. It was decorated with his own wood carvings, and paintings on the walls inside.

John Paul, the shepherd at Farringford, about 1880

Tennyson found in the Farringford shepherd the epitome of the wise, stalwart countryman, and he had endless conversations with him. He lived to be 93, dying in 1886, and he used often to dine with the Tennysons at Farringford. Tennyson doubtless had him in mind when he wrote in 'Locksley Hall Sixty Years After':

Plowmen, Shepherds, have I found, and more
    than once, and still could find,
Sons of God, and kings of men in utter
    nobleness of mind.

Most of the other farm workers and servants at Farringford were individualists, like the coachman William Knight. The farm at Farringford was a source of delight to Tennyson, who enjoyed discussing the details of agriculture with the manager and farm hands; often in moments of despair, he longed to be 'a simple country squire'.

right
Sir John Simeon, about 1867
Julia Margaret Cameron

Sir John Simeon, the squire of Swainston, became
Tennyson's closest friend of his mature years. They first
met after Lionel's christening, and thereafter rarely a
week went by when the Tennysons were on the Isle of
Wight that they did not meet, either at Farringford, out
walking, or at Swainston, some eight miles away from
Farringford. It was Simeon who urged him to work
upon the lines 'O that twere possible' which developed
into *Maud*; when Simeon died, Tennyson wrote his
poem 'In the Garden at Swainston'; of Simeon, 'The
prince of Courtesy', he wrote to Lady Simeon. 'He was
the only man on earth, I verily believe, to whom I could,
and more than once opened my whole heart, and he
has also given me, in many a conversation at
Farringford, in my little attic, his utter confidence. I
knew none like him for tenderness and generosity.'

right
Garibaldi and **Tennyson** meet at Farringford,
from the *Illustrated London News*, 23 April
1864

left
Tennyson's study at Farringford, with his
deerhound 'Lufra' in the foreground
W. Biscombe Gardner

The Prince Consort, August 1855
J. E. Mayall

The Queen's devotion to her Laureate owed much to the Prince Consort's admiration of him; on the night the letter of appointment reached him, Tennyson dreamed of the Prince, who kissed him on the cheek. He was 'Very kind, but very German'. In 1860 the Prince wrote to him, requesting an autograph in his volume of the *Idylls of the King*: 'You would thus add a peculiar value to the book, containing those beautiful songs, from the perusal of which I derived the greatest enjoyment. They quite rekindle the feelings which the legends of King Arthur must have inspired the chivalry of old. . . .' The Queen's own favourite portrait of her husband, by Robert Thorburn, was of the Prince aged 24, in black medieval armour, which was set in a jewel case in the form of a shrine; it was very much in the spirit of Tennyson's Arthurian Idyll.

Emma, Queen of the Sandwich Islands, 1865

Farringford, 28 September 1864:

Queen Emma of the Sandwich Islands arrived, Major Hopkins and a huge native, Mr. Hoapili in attendance. . . . We had had a throne made out of our Ilex wood. It was first used by the Queen. She, poor lady, wanted to stay quietly here, but she had to go to banquets etc. about the Island. . . . A. and I were pleased with her sweet dignity of manner and a calmness that made one think of an Egyptian statue.

. . . She has an affectionate nature; something very pathetic about her.

Another exotic visitor was the little Prince of Abyssinia, Alamayu, who came three years later with his guardian, Captain Speedy. The Prince on seeing the wilderness behind the house, said: 'Take care, there will be an elephant in that jungle.'

left
Alfred Tennyson, 1867
Julia Margaret Cameron

below
Maud and **Violet Tennyson,** daughters of
Horatio Tennyson, 1868
Julia Margaret Cameron

Horatio, following the death of Harriet, was bitter and
irritable. Emily noted that Maud and Violet were 'so pale
on Friday' because 'they had overheard him speaking
angrily to Miss Vernon [their governess] as he often
does. . . .'

Alfred Tennyson, about 1870
Julia Margaret Cameron

Cecilia Tennyson, Alfred's niece, Horatio's
third daughter

112

Henry Taylor (1800–86), about 1865
Julia Margaret Cameron

A noted Civil Servant in the Colonial Office, much
regarded in his day as a playwright and minor poet, Sir
Henry Taylor (knighted in 1869) is best remembered
today for his face, immortalised by Julia Margaret
Cameron in innumerable guises. Although the
Tennysons knew him from the early days of their
marriage, there was something of an edge to his
relationship with Alfred, who once told Julia Margaret,
in a spirit of not entirely gentle banter, that Taylor had
a smile like a fish. 'Yes, Alfred,' she replied, 'like a fish
when God moved upon the face of the waters.'

Benjamin Jowett (1817–93)
Julia Margaret Cameron

First come I; my name is Jowett.
There's no knowledge but I know it.
I am Master of this College:
What I don't know isn't knowledge.

(The Masque of Balliol)

It is no exaggeration to say that Jowett *was* Balliol, and
one of the great academics of the nineteenth century.
His friendship with Alfred of some forty years was of
great importance to both men; with Jowett, Tennyson
could talk freely and deeply. Both abhorred narrow
dogmatism, and Jowett was once arraigned before the
Vice-Chancellor's court in Oxford for some of his
speculations on the nature of scripture. In Jowett's
company Alfred was at his most profound, and often at
his most lighthearted.

113

above
Robert Browning (1812–89), 1868
Julia Margaret Cameron

right
Cecilia Tennyson, 1871
Julia Margaret Cameron

Tennyson told his son,

> Browning never greatly cares about the glory of
> words or beauty of form: he has told me that the
> world must take him as it finds him. As for his
> obscurity in his great imaginative analyses, I believe
> it is a mistake to explain poetry too much, people
> really have pleasure in discovering their own
> interpretations. He has a mighty intellect, but
> sometimes I cannot read him. He seldom attempts
> the marriage of sense with sound, although he
> shows a spontaneous felicity in the adaptation of
> word to ideas and feelings . . . He has plenty of music
> in him but he cannot get it out. . . .

From this it may be judged that the relationship
between the two men, so similar in some respects, was
amiable but a little guarded. In death they are closer
than in life, for Tennyson's grave in Westminster Abbey
lies beside that of Browning.

THE TENNYSONS were determined that Hallam and Lionel should grow up together, to 'be brothers indeed all their lives'. At first they were taught at home by Alfred, then by a succession of tutors, most notable of whom was Henry Graham Dakyns, who became a close friend of the family. Thereafter they went to a small school in Dorset run by Charles Kegan Paul, later Tennyson's publisher. There seemed no question but that they should go on to Marlborough. George Granville Bradley was one of the great Victorian educators, headmaster of Marlborough from 1858 to 1870, then Master of University College, Oxford, and latterly, Dean of Westminster until his death. The two families had been close since they had met in 1855 on the Isle of Wight close to Farringford, and the Bradley girls were frequent guests at the Tennyson homes. Hallam did well at Marlborough, and it was a matter of sadness that Lionel was thought too delicate to withstand the cold of Marlborough, and was sent to Eton instead. But they were reunited at Trinity College, Cambridge. Emily always felt that Lionel, who had a more errant nature than his brother, would have benefited from the close supervision of the Bradleys; Lionel seemed happy to carve his own path.

left
George Granville Bradley (1821–1903)
From the album of Lionel Tennyson

right
Lionel Tennyson, 1866
Julia Margaret Cameron

Lionel Tennyson, dressed as the Marquis de St
Cast for Mrs Cameron's production of *Payable
on Demand,* 1869
Julia Margaret Cameron

Lionel Tennyson (*right*) at Eton
From the album of Lionel Tennyson

Emily wrote to her niece Agnes Weld of her growing sons:

> However little they may have of their Father's genius they bid fair to have the childlike simplicity of his nature. It is quite touching to see my boy of 5′ 10½″ kneel by my knees and say his prayers just as he has always done. Lionel too is just the same.

But Lionel had less of Hallam's unswerving devotion to his mother and father. Edward Lear, visiting Farringford in 1866, 'loathed the brutal and snubbing way in which he [Tennyson] treated Lionel and Hallam.' Lear was a prejudiced observer, with his ambivalence towards Tennyson, but it is certain that both Alfred and Emily found Lionel less malleable than his brother.

Hallam Tennyson, 1890

Hallam devoted his life to the service of his father, both
before and after his death. He was 32 when he married,
and his wife, Audrey Boyle, must have found it difficult
to be as submissive to Alfred and Emily as he was. Of
their three sons, two were killed in the First World War.

Lionel Tennyson, about 1884
The Cameron Studio

Algernon Swinburne wrote disparagingly of Lionel in 1872: no longer 'in the May of his beauty, ere he shot up into a tall, loutish common featured youth'. If not to Swinburne's taste, Lionel became a dandy, and known for his considerable charm; he married, in 1878, Eleanor Locker, the daughter of Tennyson's friend and travelling companion, Frederick Locker. He was engaged when only 21, and the resemblance to Arthur Hallam, with a marriage only half-approved of by his parents, was made tragically closer when he died of fever in 1886, at the age of 31. He had found a post in the India Office, which made him financially independent, and achieved some success; in the autumn of 1885, he sailed to India as the guest of the Viceroy, but in his tour around the country he contracted a fever. He died on the way home and was buried at sea, on 20 April 1886.

And dreams that scarce will let me be
Not there to bid my boy farewell
When That within the coffin fell,
Fell, and flashed into the Red Sea. . . .

BY THE THIRD quarter of the century Tennyson was a figure of settled reputation, rich on the proceeds of his poetry as no other poet had been since Byron. Yet he remained as thin-skinned and sensitive to criticism as he had been when *Poems, Chiefly Lyrical* had been mangled by the reviewers forty years before. He had begun to attract parody and satire, some clever and pointed, like Swinburne's caricature of his philosophical musings, *The Higher Pantheism.*

Swinburne had responded with *The Higher Pantheism in a Nutshell*:

> One, who is not, we see: but one, who we see not, is:
> Surely this is not that: but that is assuredly this.
> What, and wherefore, and whence? for under is over and under:
> If thunder could be without lightning, lightning could be without thunder.
> . . . .
> Body and spirit are twins: God only knows which is which:
> The soul squats down in the flesh, like a tinker drunk in a ditch.
> More is the whole than a part: But half is more than the whole:
> Clearly, the soul is the body: but is not the body the soul? . . .
> God, whom we see not, is: and God, who is not, we see:
> Fiddle, we know, is diddle: and diddle, we take it, is dee.

The very skill and felicity of his writing ('Tennyson was nothing if not virtuoso', as George Bernard Shaw aciduously remarked) made it seem that he was able to turn out verse by the yard with little attention to content or feeling. Other attacks on him were more vitriolic, especially after he accepted a peerage in 1883:

> You must wake and call me early, call me early Vicky dear
> Tomorrow will be the silliest day we've seen for many a year
> For I'm a lackey and a prig, Vicky, that sham and shoddy reveres,
> And I'm to be one of the Peers, Vicky, I'm to be one of the Peers.
> *Secular Review*

Yet he had consistently refused honours over many years, and only accepted late in life in the knowledge that it would benefit Hallam, and that it was intended as an honour to the whole world of literature. Steadily Tennyson, so unestablishment a figure in his dress, manner, and many of his attitudes, came to be an epitome of Victorianism for the rising generation. For the Sitwells, children of the Victorian age, but self-consciously

MR. TENNYSON, READING "IN MEMORIAM" TO HIS SOVEREIGN

emancipated from it, he was 'Lawn Tennyson' (James Joyce's 'gentleman poet'), or in Edith
Sitwell's sibilant verses

> Alfred Lord Tennyson crossing the bar laid
> with cold vegetation from pale deputations
> of temperance workers (all signed *In Memoriam*)
> Hoping with glory to trip the Laureate's feet

(moving in classical metres) . . . .

The unblemished nobility of the figure portrayed in his son's great *Alfred Lord Tennyson. A
Memoir* (1897) begged deflation, and his reputation as a poet was mired in a great wave of
criticism. Even in Max Beerbohm's affectionate cartoon, the wild ranting poet and the
little dumpy Queen are reduced to figures of fun.

THE 'SUMMER HOUSE' at Blackdown near Haslemere, which Emily named Aldworth, was an expression of the Tennysons' revulsion for mankind 'en masse'. It would have been difficult to have found a more isoated position, or a house with a more grandiose outlook. The place chosen, Black Horse Copse, was a narrow plateau formed on the southern face of Blackdown, over 800 feet above sea level; it was as lonely as the eyrie in Tennyson's 'The Eagle':

> He clasps the crag with crooked hands:
> Close to the sun in lonely lands,
> Ring'd with the azure world, he stands.

The town of Haslemere in the valley two miles away might, in practice, have been at ten times that distance.

When they first visited the site, there was no more than a track: Emily noted in her journal for 5 June 1867:

. . . we went there in an odd procession, Lionel on a donkey with a lady's saddle, I driving in the basket-carriage, the rest walking. The wheels spun round on the axles without touching ground in some of the deep ruts, and the carriage had to be lifted over, William leading the pony carefully. At last we reached the charming ledge on the heathery down. This looks over an immense view bounded by the South-downs on the south, by Leith Hill on the north. Copse-wood surrounds the ledge, and the hill protects it from the north-west. The foxglove was in full bloom. A. helped me down the mountain-path. We all enjoyed the day thoroughly.

The architect, James Knowles, adapted their sketch and plan, and in the process he persuaded them to build something more substantial than the small country retreat they had intended.

The cottage, as he first proposed it, was to be a small square, four-roomed house, with a door in the middle, like one in which he was then staying near Haslemere. . . .

The plans for a four-roomed cottage gave way somewhat as I talked the matter over with Mr. and Mrs. Tennyson, the latter giving me certain rough ideas which she could not quite express by drawing, but which I understood enough to put into shape; and presently I went to Farringford with designs for a less un-important dwelling. It grew and grew as it was talked over and considered, the details being all discussed with Mrs. Tennyson, while he contented himself by pretending to protest against any addition and improvement.

At last, one day, when I brought sketches for an arcaded porch to complete the design, he put his foot down and said he would have nothing to do with it—that he would have no more additions—that it would ruin him and could not be entertained for a moment. He walked to and fro, coming back from time to time to the table where the drawing lay and looking at it. He admitted that he liked it more and more the more he looked at it, but presently cried out with simulated fury, 'Get thee behind me, Satan,' and ran out of the room. Then I knew that the porch was won. When it was built he got to be very fond of it, and used to call attention to the way in which the landscape was framed by the arches of it. He even had a picture of it made by a friend to show this effect.

The foundation stone was laid on 23 April 1868, Shakespeare's birthday, with Sir John Simeon, his wife and daughter, the architect and his wife as the only guests. The house took shape slowly, and the grounds much longer, with the two Tennyson boys doing much of the work with their father. Emily wrote to Thomas Woolner in October 1869:

As for ourselves we have been living for more than two months in the midst of a sandy desert, wheelbarrows continually coming and going and sometimes carts and often the strokes of the joiners' and masons' tools and later of the stone carvers. . . . We shall not finish furnishing our house this year, the finishing of the house and shaping of the grounds having taken so much longer that we expected. . . . We have no road yet to our house. . . .

The boys 'are doing the work of homey hands here on the terrace and road.' Among the early visitors, once the house and the grounds were fit to receive guests were the Gladstones, who 'frisked about like boy and girl in the heather'. Turgenev, whom Alfred much admired, 'a tall, large, white haired man with a strong face', came to stay, and told them strange stories about the Cossacks. Alfred discovered that George Eliot lived nearby, and she was thereafter to be found at Aldworth, sometimes in agreement with Tennyson, as over 'the namby Pambyism of the age, which hates a story to end in tragedy, as if the greatest moral lessons were not taught by tragedy', or more often, in profound discord. A frequent visitor to Aldworth was Francis Palgrave, and in 1887, his brother Gifford Palgrave, the noted explorer who had last visited the Tennysons at Farringford over twenty years before, came to Aldworth. After he had left, Tennyson remarked, 'I think he was the cleverest man I ever met.'

Aldworth was the home of the Tennysons' later life. By its completion both Hallam and Lionel had passed out of childhood, and from 1874, Emily's physical collapse altered the shape of their lives. Much of their Farringford life was translated there, and even the house had something of the same feel.

Aldworth

Lord Tennyson at his desk at Aldworth, 1885
C. Roberts

The picture shows two characteristic elements of
Tennyson: his love of dogs, as he strokes 'Karenina',
and the piles of books which overwhelmed Farringford,
and set fair to occupy Aldworth as well.

It was not a large house, and it repeated some of the most noticeable characteristics of Farringford. There were on the ground floor three rooms opening out of one another and facing south — drawing-room, dining-room, and between these an ante-room where the poet had dessert laid and drank his port after dinner. On the first floor were the bedrooms of himself, his wife and his son and a noble library, book-lined like that at Farringford, and decorated with large marble plaques of the Caesars, the provenance of which I have never discovered. There was no colonnade at the entrance like that at Farringford, since the length of the house lay the other way, but the corridor which ran from the front door, past the dining-room, ante-room and drawing-room (with the kitchen quarters on the opposite side), was very broad and open with the staircase coming down at the far end, so as to give Tennyson a good space to walk up and down when the weather was bad. Here, near the garden door at the west end, hung a large oil painting by Edward Lear of Pentedelata in Calabria, with a quotation from *The Palace of Art* beneath it. The garden was very simply planned. The hill rose steeply at the back of it and the copse enclosed it completely on each side, leaving only a lawn and rose garden opposite the front door and a smooth terrace along the south side of the house fronting the view. The terrace was flanked by a stone balustrade on which stood vases for flowers. Along it tall hollyhocks and Italian cypresses rose against the view — and what a view it was, whether seen from the terrace or from the higher angle of the poet's library. One looked over the tops of the trees, which covered the slope below the garden, across fifteen or twenty miles of the Sussex Weald, chequered with cornfield, meadow and woodland, to the undulating line of the South Downs, through which when the sun was at the right point in the sky, and the air clear, one could even see a gleam of the Channel thirty miles away.

left
Sketch by Alfred Tennyson for J. Knowles, showing a detail of the proposed house on Blackdown, 1867
Alfred Tennyson

But it was a home imbued with a sense of silence and tranquillity, far removed from Farringford in the days of Mrs Cameron's theatricals and endless photographic sessions. The hospitality at Aldworth was lavish, and the house usually full of guests; but more often than not, these were the now ageing friends of thirty years standing. James Knowles was a new friend and one of the great supports of Tennyson's later years. The Laureate once said to him, 'I'm very glad to have known you. It has been a sort of lift to my life.' He recorded the sedate tenor of life at Aldworth:

He usually dined rather early, at 7 or 7.30 o'clock, and Mrs. Tennyson would generally carve (or in later times Hallam), according to the old-fashioned custom. . . . and always when at home made a move for dessert to another room—the morning room at Aldworth—where he would begin his bottle [pint] of port, and with the exception of a glass or so, would finish it, talking all the time with entire geniality and abandon, and full of reminiscences of men and things. Sometimes he would recur to his grievances at the hands of his publishers. . . .

   After dessert he would retire to his study and his after-dinner pipe, which he took quite by himself, and would then come into the drawing-room, whither the others had repaired some time, and join in general talk again and perhaps read, at someone's request, some of his own poems, till the ladies left for bed. Then he would invite some favoured guest to his study. . . . At such times all his inmost thoughts and feelings, recollections and speculations of his life came out with the open simplicity of a child and the keen insight and far sight of a prophet. . . .

Aldworth, drawn in pen and ink,
19 November 1889

It was the routine of an ageing but still alert and active man, but, indubitably, one in his twilight. It is this atmosphere, permeated with the spirit of Aldworth, that Tennyson himself presented in his poem to Emily (see page 9), in dedication of his last volume of poetry *The Death of Oenone* which was published posthumously.

left

William Gifford Palgrave (1826–88), about 1868
Julia Margaret Cameron

The brother of Francis Palgrave, compiler of *The Golden Treasury*, Gifford Palgrave was an adventurer. His career was unique. He served in the Bombay Native Infantry, became a Jesuit, was a spy for Napoleon III in Arabia, and an emissary for the British government in Abyssinia. In later life he served in the consular service in Central Asia, the West Indies, the Philippines, Bulgaria and Siam. His last post was as British Minister to Uruguay, where he married, and died. In this photograph, he is dressed for his Arabian journey, the subject of his best-selling *Narrative of a Year's Journey through Central and Eastern Arabia*, published in 1865, a book more noted as a monument to man's inventiveness than as a sober record of exploration.

right

George John Douglas Campbell, Eighth Duke of Argyll (1823–1900)

The Duke of Argyll and Tennyson first met at the farewell supper for Macready, and the depth of their friendship grew with the years. Argyll was a man of deep sensitivity and scholarship, and Alfred felt at ease with him. For Hallam, Argyll recalled:

> an indication of personal friendship which was granted to me very near the close of his life. I was to return to London next morning from a visit to Aldworth. Your mother had been at dinner and bidden us goodnight as usual. When, about an hour later, your father took me up to his smoking room . . . we were surprised to find your mother lying on the sofa there. Your father expressed his astonishment and said, 'My dear, you ought to have gone to bed long ago.' Her kind reply was, 'Oh, I wished to say goodbye to the Duke again as he leaves us tomorrow morning.' At that moment, you entered the room and carried your mother off. Your father, somewhat moved as I thought, occupied himself with putting fresh coals on the fire. Then, turning to me, he said in a deep and solemn voice, without mentioning your mother's name, 'It is a tender, spiritual face, is it not?'

For a man so intensely private as Tennyson, such intimacy could only exist with the closest of friends.

William Ewart Gladstone (1809–98), in his
study at Hawarden, about 1894
J. P. Mayall

With Gladstone, Tennyson could never separate his
liking for the man and his abhorrence for some of his
ideals and political practices. Yet they had a great deal
in common, and Alfred had great respect for Gladstone's
intellect and kindness; it was Gladstone who first
broached the matter of Tennyson's peerage. The
ambivalence was remarked by Knowles. He gave a
dinner party to which Gladstone was invited, and which
Alfred refused to attend out of pique. Knowles sent
Gladstone upstairs to see Tennyson, and 'Ten minutes
later the sound of shuffling feet was heard on the
staircase and Tennyson and Gladstone came into the
room arm in arm. Soon they were seated side by side on
the sofa, discussing Greek mythology.' Later that night
Tennyson remarked, 'I'm sorry I said all those hard
things about the old man.' But the next morning he
exploded with 'I never said anything bad enough about
the old rascal!'

De Vere, Aubrey Thomas (1814–1902)
Julia Margaret Cameron

Born into an Anglo-Irish family of some note in Limerick, Aubrey de Vere was educated at Trinity College, Dublin, and published his first major poem, *The Waldenses*, at the age of 28. Like many of his caste, he became an emotional captive of Celtic Ireland, although in his case it went so far as causing him to abandon his family's Protestantism for the Roman Catholic Church. It says much for the closeness of his friendship for Tennyson, who had a deep suspicion for Catholicism, that his conversion passed with little comment. Alfred found in him a stimulating and refreshing companion, especially on their visit to Ireland in 1849, and a staunch friend. He managed to convey to Tennyson something of the passion he felt for Celtic legend and literature, a commitment which caused Matthew Arnold to remark: 'Nothing perhaps did more to help the Celtic revival than Aubrey de Vere's tender insight into the Irish character.'

Frederick Locker-Lampson (1821–95)
Julia Margaret Cameron

Locker, like so many of Tennyson's younger friends, submitted his work to him, and it was the origin of a lasting friendship. He took Tennyson on a short visit to Paris in 1870, which both enjoyed, although Alfred remarked, as one evening they sat in the gallery of a Parisian theatre with barely a view of the stage, 'Locker, this is like being stuck on a spike in Hell.' On the return journey, Alfred, who was as absent-minded on occasion as he was short-sighted, left his old cloak, some thirty years old, in the railway carriage. He told Locker that he could have it if he cared to retrieve it from the Lost Property Office, which he did; it is now, together with one of Tennyson's travelling hats, in the Usher Gallery in Lincoln (*overleaf*).

Wash drawing of *Enoch Arden's* Island, about
1880
Edward Lear

Alfred Tennyson's cloak and hat

137

Campagna di Roma, Italy
Edward Lear

I am a part of all that I have met;
Yet all experience is an arch wherethro'
Gleams that untravelled world, whose margin fades
For ever and for ever when I move.
How dull it is to pause, to make an end,
To rust unburnish'd, not to shine in use!
As tho' to breathe were life.

Ulysses

Edward Lear (1812–88)
From the album of Lionel Tennyson

Prickly, easily wounded and conscious of his physical
defects, Lear often succumbed to Alfred's bullying ill-
temper, when other men would have brushed it aside.
Yet he revered Alfred's work, and adored Emily and her
sons; he even named a house the Villa Tennyson. Yet he
alone of the many illustrators of Tennyson's poetry
caught the muscularity and strength of the writing.
Alfred loathed the Illustrated Edition of his work, and did
not much care for the photographs Julia Margaret
Cameron produced for the *Idylls of the King.* Lear's great
project for illustrating Tennyson was only partially
accomplished, but the power of his drawings is evident
in the few shown here.

138

above
Pass of Tempe, Greece
Edward Lear

'The long divine Peneian pass.'

Wady Feiràn, Sinai
Edward Lear

'Imbowered vaults of pillared palm.'

Akrokeraunian Mountains, Albania
Edward Lear

'The vast Akrokeraunian walls.'

The Passing of King Arthur
From Illustrations to Tennyson's *Idylls of the King*, 1875

Julia Margaret Cameron

HENRY TAYLOR, a friend to the Tennysons from the early years of their marriage, remarked of Alfred in 1860: 'He wants a story to treat, being full of poetry with nothing to put it in.' It was this search for a theme of sufficient weight to challenge his skill that led Tennyson to devote so much of his later years to historical drama. He aimed to 'portray the making of England', from the Anglo-Saxons and Normans, with plays like *Harold* and *Becket*, to adding the coda to Shakespeare's history plays, with *Queen Mary.* They contained much fine verse, but little sense of stagecraft: indeed he intended that they should be quarried by actors and managements, rather than performed as he wrote them. What success *Becket*, in particular, achieved owed as much to the skill of the actor manager, Henry Irving, as to Tennyson's mighty lines. But the plays are evidence of tremendous energy, quite unlike the picture of the ailing, gloomy old man he often liked to convey. He grumbled constantly about his shortsightedness, and even in 1890 after he had gone with James Knowles to see the noted oculist, Sir Andrew Clark, and Clark was able to 'pronounce favourably on him', he retorted, 'No man shall persuade me I'm not going blind.' Petty fears and doubts could unnerve him, but he seemed able to survive true crises. In 1886, he suffered the annihilating blow of Lionel's death on board a ship returning from India. 'The thought of it tears me to pieces,' he said, 'he was so young and full of promise . . .'; but he recovered, and, as in the years after the death of Arthur Hallam, seemed to gain new force in his writing. Three years later he fell ill, and sunk so low that he was not expected to recover. He took grim delight in denying the doctors' prognosis that he would never rise from his bed again, and he was soon seen stumping the downs at Farringford, and at Aldworth, with his nurse, Emma Durham, in tow. But some of the old, energy seemed to have gone: Bishop Boyd Carpenter noted: 'His manner was quiet, and he was, shall I say, *gentler* than before.'

Sir Henry Irving (1838–1905)

Irving, the doyen of the English stage, produced Tennyson's plays and created a stage script from his verse. One motive for his espousal of Tennyson as a playwright was that he was short of substantial leading parts in which to display his talents; Tennyson's style of drama allowed him full scope.

To Lady Tennyson
with love and
greeting from Benjamin Jowett
1893.

Alfred Tennyson, 1888
Barraud

Eleanor Locker, widow of Lionel Tennyson,
about 1886

Alfred accepted Eleanor as the daughter of his old friend,
Frederick Locker, but after Lionel's death he was
dismayed that she intended to remarry, and within two
years of Lionel's death, to Augustine Birrell. 'Why do
you want to force an entrance into my family?' was his
daunting first remark to the young man. But Birrell was
devoted to Lionel's two sons, and Tennyson's objections
melted.

Audrey Boyle, wife of **Hallam Tennyson,**
August 1884
H. S. Mendelssohn

A notable Irish beauty, Audrey Boyle first came to visit
Tennyson with her aunt, Mary Boyle, the artist and
novelist. She and Hallam were married in June 1884, in
Henry VII's Chapel, in Westminster Abbey. Hallam's
devotion to his father was obsessional, and life must
have been difficult for Audrey in a household of which
she was not fully mistress. But Alfred had a great
affection for her, which she reciprocated.

left
Alfred, Lord Tennyson, August 1892
Lowes Dickinson

The charcoal drawing is inscribed 'To Lady Tennyson in
memory of days at Aldworth, August and September
1892.' The energy of this portrait contrasts with the
frailty shown in other pictures and in the descriptions of
those who met Tennyson in his last weeks.

right
Lord Tennyson with his nurse on Freshwater
Down, 1889
Reginald Cleaver

Tennyson's nurse had suggested that he write a hymn
of thanksgiving to celebrate his recovery. One evening,
she went into his room to light the candles, and he
thrust a paper before her. 'Will this do for you, old
woman?' he said, and read his poem, *Crossing the Bar*; it
seemed to her that he had written his own death song.
Hallam noted:

> 'Crossing the Bar' was written in my father's eighty-
> fourth year, on a day in October when we came from
> Aldworth to Farringford. Before reaching Farringford
> he had the Moaning of the Bar in his mind and after
> dinner he showed me the poem written out. I said,
> 'That is the crown of your life's work.' He answered,
> 'It came in a moment.'

'Karenina', Lord Tennyson's Siberian
Wolfhound
From the album of Lionel Tennyson

148

Lord and **Lady Tennyson**, with **Hallam
Tennyson**, 1892
The Cameron Studio

This is the last photograph of Tennyson and his family.

IF TENNYSON in his eighties seemed imperishable, the sense of death was all around him as his friends and family were whittled away. Henry Taylor died in the same year as Lionel, his sister Emily, the year after; Edward Lear, Browning and William Allingham followed on, with poor, mad Edward Tennyson dying in 1890.

It was not until the autumn of 1892, in the weeks after his eighty-third birthday, that Tennyson's energy failed him; Bram Stoker, who was Irving's manager, found him 'grand but broken'. Hallam at his father's request set out at the beginning of September for Lincolnshire to see the old rectory at Somersby, then on the point of being sold. When he returned on 22 September he was shocked at the deterioration in his father's condition. But Tennyson showed amazing resilience. He continued to receive friends, among them Benjamin Jowett, and on 24 September, came down for dinner as of old. His critical sense was still sharp when he discussed the forthcoming production of *Becket* with Bram Stoker, and went through the proofs of *The Death of Oenone*: he even went for a drive to Haslemere with Hallam. But by 4 October he was clearly dying and on the next day, Wednesday:

His last food was taken at a quarter to four, and he tried to read, but could not. He exclaimed, 'I have opened it.' Whether this referred to the Shakespeare, opened by him at

'Hang there like fruit, my soul,
Till the tree die'

which he always called among the tenderest lines in Shakespeare: or whether one of his last poems, of which he was fond, was running through his head I cannot tell.

On that evening, sunset came at 5.25, and the full moon rose at a quarter to six:

. . . the full moon flooded the room and the great landscape outside with light; and we watched in solemn stillness. His patience and quiet strength had power upon those who were nearest and dearest to him; we felt thankful for the love and the utter peace of it all; and his own lines of comfort from 'In Memoriam' were strongly borne in upon us. He was quite restful, holding my wife's hand, and, as he was passing away, I spoke over him his own prayer, 'God accept him! Christ receive him!' because I knew that he would have wished it.

Lord Tennyson, in his skullcap, autumn 1892
Cameron and Smith

This shows Tennyson as Bram Stoker described him in his last days, with his long black hair falling thin and straggling from under his skull cap.

152

'Nothing to quicken the darkness but the light of the full moon.'

The death of Lord Tennyson, with Audrey
Tennyson, Dr Dabbs, and Hallam Tennyson at
the bedside

The unveiling of the Tennyson Memorial on Freshwater Down, 6 August 1897
F. N. Broderick

left

G. F. Watts working on the Tennyson statue on 3 August 1903
Christopher Turner

The statue, which stands near the Chapter House of Lincoln Cathedral, was unveiled in July 1905.

right

Alfred Tennyson
W. Jeffrey

Crossing the Bar.

—

Sunset & evening star,
    And one clear call for me.
And may there be no moaning of the bar,
    When I put out to sea,

But such a tide as moving seems asleep,
    Too full for sound & foam,
When that which drew from out the boundless deep
    Turns again home.

Twilight & evening bell,
    And after that the dark!
And may there be no sadness of farewell,
    When I embark!

For tho' from out our bourne of Time & Place
    The flood may bear me far,
I hope to see my Pilot face to face,
    When I have crost the bar.

Crossing the Bar
Manuscript

Sources

Text sources

I have not given source references for the individual quotations in this book, since they are drawn for the most part from three essential works for any study of Tennyson.

Alfred, Lord Tennyson. By his Son, is Hallam Tennyson's supreme memorial to his father. First published in 1897, it has appeared in many editions. Its great merit is that Hallam culled the memories of his father's friends and contemporaries, and includes many conversations with Alfred Tennyson himself. The *Materials* for the life were privately printed, and his own drafts is in the Tennyson Research Centre in Lincoln. It is also obsessively discreet.

Alfred Tennyson by his grandson Charles Tennyson. Until Sir Charles Tennyson published his splendid life of Alfred Tennyson, the poet's reputation languished. He explored all the areas which Hallam had shunned in a biography of outstanding skill and compulsive readability. First published by Macmillan in 1949, it went to a reprinted edition in 1950, and a new edition in 1968. It was also supplemented by a lifetime's work by Sir Charles, in articles, pamphlets and other books, which are listed in a bibliography of his work published by The Tennyson Society. It is the *fons et origo* of Tennyson studies.

Tennyson by Christopher Ricks is a necessary complement to Sir Charles's work, for it explains the real importance and limitations of Tennyson as a poet, as well as amplifying the details of his life with full reference to the original sources among the family papers. It is a testing and entirely fulfilling book to read, which locates, dissects, and then re-assembles the subtleties of Tennyson's poetry. Published by Macmillan in 1972, it is a modern classic.

For those who wish to delve further, R. W. Rader has some very interesting insights into Tennyson's early life in *Tennyson's Maud: The Biographical Genesis* (University of California Press, Berkeley and Los Angeles, 1963). Hallam Tennyson produced a further volume of memories by his father's contemporaries: *Alfred Tennyson and his Friends* (Macmillan, 1911). H. D. Rawnsley produced *Memories of the Tennysons* (James MacLehose, Glasgow, 1900). A selection of Lady Tennyson's letters has been published by James O. Hoge (The Pennsylvania State University Press, Philadelphia and London, 1974), while the vast bulk of the Tennyson correspondence has been fully explored by

Professor Robert Martin for his comprehensive new life of Tennyson, which is forthcoming shortly. The best edition of Tennyson's poems is that edited by Christopher Ricks (Longmans, 1969), while an annotated *Bibliography of Alfred Tennyson* was published by Charles Tennyson and Christine Fall (University of Georgia Press, Athens, Georgia, 1967).

The author and publishers are grateful to the following:

Chatto & Windus for permission to quote from *Stars and Markets*, by Sir Charles Tennyson
Major A. E. Tennyson d'Eyncourt and the Lincolnshire Archives Office for permission to quote from the Tennyson d'Enycourt Papers
Lord Tennyson and the Lincolnshire Library Service for permission to quote from material in the Tennyson Research Centre

Picture sources

The author and publishers are grateful to the following for permission to reproduce the photographs listed:

By Gracious Permission of Her Majesty The Queen: page 108
Country Life: page 43
National Monument Record: pages 126–7
National Portrait Gallery: pages 53, 56, 57, 58, 59, 60, 133, 135 (*right*), 150
The Tennyson Research Centre, Lincoln, by permission of Lord Tennyson and the Lincolnshire Library Service: all other photographs
Endpapers by Peter Foster, Horncastle